Praise for A Sac[

Burke creates an entire leadership ecosystem for the reader; one that is original and yet familiar, and most importantly, accessible. *A Sacred Trust* is a great resource for any leader who wants to more fully express themselves in the world.

Andy Churgin, Founding Partner, Chain Reaction Partners

In *A Sacred Trust*, Burke offers an inspiring vision and pathway for powerful transformation which brings to life our inherent brilliance. What strikes me is that this path is based not on a sense of lack or incompleteness, but on a view of our fundamental worthiness and wholeness. Page after page I am lifted into a bigger vision of what is possible for us as individuals and as humanity. Burke's direct language and practical guidance bring lofty ideals into real-world application. This book is a treasure for anyone dedicated to uplifting themselves and others in service to our world.

Charlotte Z. Rotterdam, MTS, Faculty and Director, Center for the Advancement of Contemplative Education, Naropa University

Burke has synthesized into this elegant guide a life changing experience that I personally went through with him a decade ago. So much of who I am and the mission I am leading has been influenced by the concepts in this book. It is a testament to Burke's leadership and his impact on so many others to translate a deeply personal transformation into a self-directed guide.

John D. Anderson, entrepreneur, executive advisor, and author of *Replace Retirement – Living Your Legacy in the Exponential Age*

In *A Sacred Trust*, Burke brings two rivers together: the poetic and the practical. He invites the reader into a life of excellence and meaning, and provides the map for the journey we all must take to realize our brilliance.

Craig Ross, CEO, Verus Global, and author of *Do Big Things*

A Sacred Trust is an exciting and profound contribution to the growing wave of comprehensive human development in education. By 2020, more than 400 schools, 150,000 students, and thousands of educators will be using our charter school system's Compass Model, inspired directly by Burke's four disciplines. No matter what profession you're in, if you are committed to your growth as a leader, I highly recommend this book. Its contents, and Burke's counsel, have enriched my life immeasurably.

Todd Dickson, CEO, Valor Collegiate Academies

A step to the side is sometimes all it takes to transform an average view out of the window into a breathtaking landscape. If that breathtaking landscape is who you can be in the world, Burke's Four Disciplines can help you with the window, the frame to see your own best potential, and with the practices, the steps, that will help you access that potential. I have never regretted to use Burke's frame to consider my reality in a different way. As simple as it seems, it works for me beyond measure.

Cécile Coutens, President, Royal Canin Americas

In *A Sacred Trust*, Burke lays out a compelling vision of an expansive life we can choose to live, along with practical tools to free ourselves from living small. In a style that is deeply inspirational while fiercely action focused, the book's pages are overflowing with wisdom that has helped me immensely in my relationships at home and at work.

Mark Cadman, Managing Director, EVP at BBDO Worldwide

I believe that with clear minds and open hearts—and full self-awareness and responsibility for all our choices in every moment—leaders and all human beings can create extraordinary possibilities together, and a world that works for us all. *A Sacred Trust* is a fresh, thought provoking, and transformational guidebook on that path.

Robert Krenza, CEO and Founder, BlackWolf Consultants Inc.

Burke has been my guide on the path of self-discovery, renewal, and growth as a leader for more than a decade. His book, born of years of experience, is true to what makes him a powerful coach and stellar human being. Reading *A Sacred Trust*, I felt invited into the depths of my own internal wisdom. More importantly than having answers, Burke asks the right questions to help you find the brilliance of your own path of leadership. His Four Disciplines give you a way to orient your actions with inspiration and consciousness, and live with purpose and passion. In short—to boldly be your fullest self.

Dale Johnson, Head of School, The Field School

A Sacred Trust

THE FOUR DISCIPLINES OF CONSCIOUS LEADERSHIP

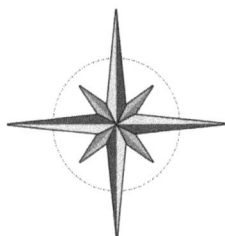

BURKE MILLER

White Wolf Wisdom Press
Boulder, Colorado

Library of Congress Control Number: 2019904982
Print ISBN 978-1-7330063-0-9
Ebook ISBN 978-1-7330063-1-6
Copyright information available upon request.

Cover Design: Heather Corbin, Corbin Creative
Cover image: Simon Migaj/Unsplash
Editor: John Kadlecek
Interior Design: J. L. Saloff

v. 1.00
First Edition, 2019
Printed on acid free paper in the USA.

To the Four Daughters of Beauty

To Ryan

To Sandra

Contents

Foreword
by Mark Gerzon

OVER THE PAST 50 YEARS, I have written several books on the topic of leadership, and personally coached leaders in settings ranging from school systems to complex organizations; from the United States House of Representatives to political party leaders in Africa, the Middle East, and Asia. Throughout that time, I have observed that our ability to make progress collectively on the big issues of our times has always depended on our willingness to look at ourselves in the mirror.

In my book *Global Citizens*, I observe:

> *As a species we face a choice about whether or not we will invest in developing our global intelligence. If we do not raise our collective global intelligence, we may close our eyes and become blind, close our minds and become rigid, close our hearts and become callous, close our hands and become aggressive. History shows that we human beings have both the capacity to open our eyes, minds, hearts, and hands—and to close them. We have the capacity to build an interdependent, peaceful global civilization, as well as splinter and fragment into endless conflict. We can see the world narrowly or broadly, depending on which*

parts of ourselves we are able to develop. Indeed, wherever we
may live, the drama of the Earth itself is occurring within each
of us.

It is in this context—of looking within ourselves to our own hearts, minds, and hands, in order to build a better world—that I find *A Sacred Trust* to be so wise and useful. The world urgently needs Burke Miller's approach to developing ourselves as leaders and human beings. The four disciplines he describes are the antidote to demagoguery, commercialism, and egotism that parade as "leadership" in many countries today.

We live in a world where finger pointing and polarization are too often the norm. If we are paying attention, we all see it on the news and in our workplaces. In *A Sacred Trust*, Burke goes to the root of the ways of being that generate the negativity and unproductive conflict we experience in our lives. While there are many books that offer fixes to the problems we see around us, Burke takes a different approach. Instead, he helps us see and seize the opportunity we each have to work with the conflicts that live *inside* of us. With compassion, Burke invites us to use our shadow sides—like arrogance, defensiveness, control, and judgment—as doorways of awareness. From the very beginning, *A Sacred Trust* acknowledges that we cannot reach the light if we do not face the darkness.

I have been fortunate to experience Burke's work—and these disciplines—personally. When Burke invited me to experience his coaching process, I was profoundly moved by the two-day journey. Instead of staying on the surface of my own leadership challenges, it took me into the marrow of my life.

A Sacred Trust is a deep dive to the heart of what it means to be an effective and fulfilled human being. As a lifelong student of depth psychology and a wide range of wisdom traditions, I clearly recognize and resonate with Burke's masterful synthesis and integration of the insight offered by indigenous wisdom, contemporary psychology, basic neuroscience, and leadership practice.

More than theory, *A Sacred Trust* is a provocative guide to self-development. It is present in Burke's journaling questions, the way he connects you to universal archetypes, and the elegant framework into which he invites his readers. One of my favorite elements in this book that punctuate the text every few pages are the "Paradigm Shift Alerts." These contrasting statements, which juxtapose old paradigm ideas about leadership with new ones, symbolize the mission of this book: to provide a vision of leadership that is worthy of our times.

Perhaps the most valuable contribution of this book however, is connecting leadership and personal growth. On the one hand, this is a book for leaders—men and women in positions of institutional authority. Whether a business executive or a university administrator or a civic leader, those who have organizational responsibilities will find the four disciplines to be a professional compass for navigating a wider range of leadership challenges. On the other hand, *A Sacred Trust* is equally valuable for individual "seekers" who are navigating the challenges of their personal lives. Witnessing and embracing whatever crossroads we are approaching through this fourfold lens enhances our vision and reveals the right path for each of us.

This connection Burke makes between leadership and personal growth is important because it invites you to engage with leadership as a practice and a way of life, rather than a job. *A Sacred Trust* is based on the premise that who we *are*, and how we *lead*, are inextricably intertwined. Being a better *leader*, and being a better *person*, go hand in hand.

As you further your own practice of leadership, dear reader, my wish for you is that this book will evoke empowered attunement to your spirit, courageous opening of your heart, sharpened clarity of mind and honor and integrity in your actions. What our planet and humanity need most right now is leaders who are willing to do the *inner* work required to do the *outer* work of creating the kind of world we know is possible.

Mark Gerzon, author of *Global Citizens*
and *Leading through Conflict*
Boulder, Colorado

Preface

THE GREATEST PLEASURE IN MY WORK is connecting deeply with amazing human beings who care and are curious.

In a coaching conversation with the president of a multibillion-dollar global company, he shared with me the challenges he was having with a few members of his board of directors. At one point I asked him, "Who do you really work for?" He went silent for a few seconds, and then started talking about tens of thousands of employees and their families, hundreds of millions of customers around the world, and the resources of the planet itself. The passion and commitment in his voice was palpable. It was clear to both of us that while he had obvious financial, legal, and hierarchical commitments to his board, there was a much deeper answer to the question of who he worked for. What truly inspired and motivated him had little to do with the board of directors, who they were, or what they said or did. In the broader picture, he had a much larger constituency—the people and planet he was engaged with in a sacred trust.

This book is inspired by that conversation and literally thousands of conversations like it. It is about the sacred trust that we each have with ourselves, each other, and our world, no matter who we are or what we do in life. We have a relatively short time on this planet, with no idea how long it will last, and yet we rarely live like we know that's true. But what if we did? Imagine having the kind of relationship with your life where you are intensely paying attention and being fiercely intentional in the way you create your experience.

To engage with life in this way is deeply personal. It should be. It needs to be. And at the same time it is more than personal. The way we lead our lives matters in the context of a global community and a world in need of both healing and celebrating.

To hold life as something sacred and entrusted to you puts you on a path characterized by an uncommon depth of respect for yourself and your world. That mindset—of seeing your life as sacred in a world that is hungry for your gifts—elevates the quality of your presence by infusing it with the self-awareness and ways of being necessary for positive change to occur.

We live in a time that calls for all people of good heart and strong spirit to lead. This is not a time to sit on the sidelines or be a passenger. No matter what you are doing in life, show up in a way that inspires. Go for excellence. Go for achievement. But don't stop there. Do what you can to raise the level of human consciousness in the world.

If that intrigues you, if you know in yourself the calling to contribute to human motivation and capability to create a better world, then this is a book for you. It is a book for you because it offers a blueprint, a path forward, that honors the wisdom that is built into your nature. It calls forth ways of being that you intuitively know in yourself and strengthens your connection to them.

You're already on the journey. Enjoy!

Introduction

IT'S THE SUMMER OF 1967 and I am 8 years old. There is just a touch of light left in the sky on this Saturday evening in July in the deep woods of Maine. I'm sitting in a circle in a small clearing, cross-legged on the ground with 80 other boys. Only the crackling of a bonfire blazing in the center of our council ring breaks the silence.

We are waiting, barely breathing. Suddenly from out of the woods, four men burst into our midst, bare chests heaving, faces painted in bold designs of white and black.

They stop dead still, each standing tall in one of the four directions in complete silence. Then one speaks. His stern voice hits me like thunder. "I am the Wind from the East—a black feather winner knows his ability comes from Spirit." There is a pause. Another man speaks. "I am the Wind from the West—a black feather winner lives with integrity."

The Four Winds continue to speak. "I am the Wind from the South—a black feather winner acts with courage." "I am the Wind from the North—a black feather winner sees the good in all."

Their fierce voices fade out, the dead silence of the night returns, and with as much force as they came the Four Winds disappear into the woods. As their words reverberate in our ears, a council leader commands that we take to heart what we have heard and do our best to live these qualities every day.

In that moment at the council fire, so awed by the Four Winds, I heard the first whispers of the message that would become the theme of this book—two simple truths that have stayed with me throughout my life:

1) It matters to the world that we live our lives consciously—fully responsible for our experience and impact.

2) There is a fourfold pattern and symmetry to life—and to human consciousness—that supports us in being our most awake and powerfully expressed selves.

My love affair with this fourfold pattern of consciousness has spanned fifty years. It keeps coming around in various forms. I have known it as the four directions, the four seasons of human development, the four elements, the four daughters of beauty, the four archetypes of the mature human psyche, and now as the Four Disciplines of Conscious Leadership.

The Four Disciplines represent a synthesis of worldviews sourced from multiple streams of wisdom—starting with ancient Native American cosmology; building on the deep study of human nature found in the groundbreaking work of Carl Jung, transpersonal psychology, and esoteric astrology; and drawing on my forty years of professional engagement with human development and leadership principles gleaned from the teachings and insights of many brilliant thinkers, philosophers, writers, business leaders, and educators.

Given the four-year journey of writing this book and where I am now after twenty years as a leadership educator and coach, it's both fascinating and humbling to look back on the seeds planted in that early summer camp experience in Maine. The Four Winds that came crashing through the woods that night were 20-year-old camp counselors. They most likely did not fully grasp the nature of the wisdom underlying the universal energies they were tapping into. Nevertheless, they awakened something in me that has grown into a powerful thread in a lifelong love affair with the tapestry called philosophy.

I admit it—unapologetically—I am a philosopher. Always have been. A lover of wisdom, which is what the word philosophy means (philo—love, and Sophia—wisdom). I'm forever curious and driven by the question of how we should live. It's what has led me here to you—and likely you here to me.

This book is a moment in time in my understanding of what leading a life of wisdom looks like. It is one description, one path, of the philosophy and practice of approaching life and leadership as a sacred trust.

A Sacred Trust

Consider the notion that our lives are *entrusted to us* by Life itself, by all living things on the planet, and by past, present, and future generations of humans. We are each entrusted with the sacred gift of being alive, and we're meant to honor that trust by doing what we can to make a positive difference in our world.

That trust calls on a deep and balanced wisdom in us. When someone entrusts something to you, and when you hold that trust as sacred, you call on something deeper in yourself in order to deliver. Athletes call it *digging deep*. There is an expansion of yourself, a reservoir of potential and resourcefulness that you tap into when you orient to life and leadership as a sacred trust. You call on yourself to be acutely aware of what is needed in your world and show up for it in a way that is uncommonly committed. The world is hungry for people who ask themselves, "What is the world I inhabit and love, and what does that world need from me?"

Take a moment right now to imagine what that world is for you. Your home, your work, your leadership team, your marriage, and your children's lives can all be aspects of your world—yours to define. The best and most noble in you is devoted to contributing to that world—and not from a sense of obligation or indebtedness, but with a sense of privilege, pleasure, honor, and adventure.

A sacred trust goes two ways. Not only are we *entrusted by life*, but also meant to *trust in life*. Not in the sense that we trust life to take care of us in any kind of anthropomorphic and personal way. But exactly the opposite—in the sense that we trust life to be 100% neutral. We trust life to be faithful, as it has for eons, to its cycles of energy exchange, growth, diversity, decay and death without taking sides.

In the fall of 2016 I took time off from my work to travel with my wife and two close friends—a sabbatical, both an outer adventure and inner journey. Hiking up the backside of Machu Picchu with two Peruvian guides, embodying wisdom way beyond their age—in fact, imbued with wisdom centuries old—we stopped to rest and take in the energy of an ancient Inca ruin. The conversation turned philosophical, discussing the sacred nature of life on the planet and our human participation in it. One of our guides fixed his penetrating gaze on the four of us and said, "nothing is yours, and everything is for you."

Those words struck a chord in me that will probably never stop reverberating. They remain in my brain as a reminder of an essential aspect of what a sacred trust means. We are not entitled. Nor are we victims. We are not owners of this world. We are participants in the incredible possibilities and abundance that surround us. We are not here to get, but to honor. "Everything is for you." It is all there for us to be in relationship with. Our trust in possibility, abundance, and the neutrality of life is a sacred trust.

Conscious Leadership

There is a movement afoot. I don't know how big it is, but I know it exists because I can touch it in myself, and I see it in those I am close to, including my many clients.

I call this movement conscious leadership. It's a waking up to both the urgency and the absolute joy of bringing exquisite attention to our days. And right next to that attention, intensely focused intention to enrich the experience of our lives on this amazing planet.

Conscious leadership has an energy of deep devotion, fierce commitment, and firm stance. It is as much feminine as masculine, balancing gentleness, receptivity, strength and penetration.

Conscious leadership has two interconnected dimensions. One dimension is *positional*, meaning occupying a leadership role in a community, family, or organization. Another is *leading your life* in a way that creates the experience and impact you want to have. All effective positional leadership grows in the soil of leading yourself well. In other words, how you lead others is an outgrowth of your inner growth as a human being. This book addresses both aspects of conscious leadership—occupying your leadership roles well and leading your life well.

I have taught and coached hundreds of leaders around the world from nearly twenty different countries. We're always exploring how the inner journey as a human being is impacting their effectiveness inside an organization. Every leader I coach has a drive to achieve something beyond business results. Each, whether articulating it this way or not, is hungry to grow as a conscious human being—hungry to discover and activate more of their potency to create a fulfilling experience of life for themselves and make a positive difference in the lives of others.

What defines a conscious leader is commitment to self-awareness, and to being willing and able to use your power, both personal and positional, to contribute to the world.

CLARITY
Holding Empowering Narratives
Valuing Diverse Perspectives
Expanding Your Vision

INTEGRITY
Being Honest
Bringing Excellence
Caring for Your
    Physical World

Radical
Responsibility

INSPIRATION
Claiming Your Core Identity
Sourcing from Beauty
Activating Enthusiam

COURAGE
Leaning In
Braving Connection
Living in Appreciation

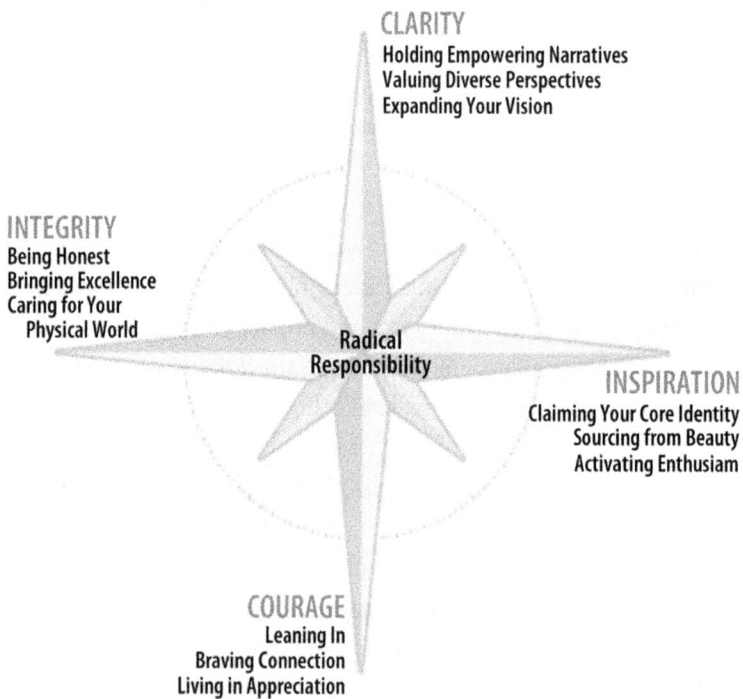

The architecture of A Sacred Trust is Radical Responsibility,
empowered by the Four Disciplines and their Core Practices

How to Get the Most Value from This Book

See the Architecture

There is a kind of sacred geometry—or perhaps *geography* would be a better word—to the Four Disciplines. The architecture of this book—the layout of conscious leadership—is a circle, not a line. The leadership journey laid out here does not have a beginning, middle, and end. It has concentric circles, beginning with the center and rippling out from there.

In Part I, chapter One defines the center, which is radical responsibility, including the core concepts of Discipline and Distortion. Chapter Two gives you an overview of the Four Disciplines themselves.

In Part II, chapters Three through Six dive more deeply into each of the Disciplines, exploring the three primary practices that activate each Discipline, and the distortions that detract from your effectiveness. Chapter Seven brings the Disciplines all together in a way that makes the whole simple and engaging to practice.

Pay Attention to the Chapter Beginnings and Endings

Take the time to do the short warm-ups at the beginning of each chapter and study the summary points at the end of each chapter.

The warm-up questions prepare your mind for what's to come, like soil for seeds. They heighten your curiosity, making your mind more receptive. The summary points help put your mind at ease—with a reassurance that remembering a few key ideas is enough.

At the end of each chapter you will find sentence completions to stimulate reflection. I invite you to take the time to write out your responses. Taking this time to reflect and write will greatly enhance your reading. It puts your mind on active alert, rather than in a more passive state. It also evokes your own wisdom, increasing the book's personal relevance and usefulness.

Reflect on the Paradigm Shifts

Merriam Webster defines paradigm shift as "an important change that happens when the usual way of thinking about or doing something is replaced by a new and different way."

This book offers potential paradigm shifts—in other words, changes from a conventional way of thinking to a new view. I highlight them throughout in boxes like the one below, labeled *Paradigm Shift Alert*.

PARADIGM SHIFT ALERT

From: Leadership is primarily a matter of positional authority.

To: Leadership is primarily a way of life, wherever you are, whomever you're with, including, and perhaps especially, in positions of authority.

Use the Activation Questions

An activation question is a highly effective self-coaching technique. It is a question that triggers your mind into a more thoughtful level of consciousness, or motivates you to take a more empowering action.

Activation questions imbed the Disciplines in you by bringing your attention to what is needed in any given moment. Asking yourself questions is provocative and compelling. Questions evoke more from you. They keep you awake, conscious, and engaged.

One of the things that makes an activation question powerful is that it has wisdom—an empowering mindset, value, or worldview—imbedded in it. Just asking yourself the question immediately creates a more conscious state of being. For example, you could ask yourself, "What is the most authentic thing I could say or do right now?" Imbedded in the question is the value of authenticity and a reminder to be authentic.

ACTIVATION QUESTIONS (EXAMPLES)
- How are the choices I'm making in this moment creating the experience of life I'm having?
- What is my world asking of me now that I am enthusiastically willing to give?

Connect to the Archetypal Energies

Earlier in my career, I worked for several years as a senior facilitator for a small but very successful leadership education company. One evening during my training to be a facilitator, I was out to dinner with the company president. We were discussing aspects of great facilitation, and he said to me in his direct but compassionate way, "To be successful with us, you're going to have to be less Boulder and more New York."

I got it immediately. It was the perfect way for him to describe not a technique, but an energy. Boulder people are seen as laid-back. He was asking me to bring more New York—with more edge, volume, and gusto.

Archetypes create an image in your mind, as well as a feeling in you, of an energetic signature like "more New York." They describe in one or two words a whole constellation of attitudes, skills, and ways of being. Archetypes are types of human beings that are universally recognized as having certain characteristics.

For example, "the queen" is an archetype. While there are few actual queens left in the world, many women embody "queen energy," as men may embody the "king" archetype. Other examples of archetypes include adventurer, wise woman, magician, teacher, mother, poet, sage, business tycoon, healer, monk, warrior, seductress, etc.. We all have these archetypes in us to some degree. The Four Disciplines help you to become aware of a well-rounded cast of characters, or archetypes, that you already embody, and others that you want to develop.

At the beginning of each of the Discipline chapters in Part II (chapters three through six) are short introductions to two archetypes that most essentially embody the energy of that Discipline. Take a moment at the beginning of those chapters to visualize and feel what these archetypes are like, and the degree to which you are familiar with them and have access to their particular energy.

Keep It Simple and Relevant

The book revolves around four disciplines. Taken together, these disciplines lay out a leadership journey that is intended to be both exciting and elegantly simple.

All we really have to remember here is four words—Inspiration, Integrity, Courage, and Clarity—four deep and multi-layered wells of wisdom to drink from for the rest of your life. If you find yourself being overwhelmed at any point in the book by too many ideas, you may find it helpful to simply stop reading, and go back to the Four Disciplines and pick one to reflect on. Ask yourself, "How is this Discipline a relevant and useful guide in my life right now? Stay with that question until your curiosity leads you back to the book.

> *I cannot stress this point enough. the Four Disciplines, and*
> *the power in them, are bigger and deeper than anything*
> *I can say about them. So please take this book as a jumping*
> *off place in your exploration, not the final word.*

Years ago, a friend and I were immersed in a conversation about life, when he paused for a moment and said, "You know, really, when you come down to it, it's not what you know, it's what you live." That's true for the ideas in this book. The key is to live them. Put them to the test of your experience and do your best to live the ones that most deeply resonate with you.

Be Both Gentle and Fierce with Yourself

The Disciplines will challenge you to be your best self. They will invite you to stretch. And as you fiercely stretch toward your best self, it's important to keep in mind that you are doing the best you can at any given moment or phase of your life.

A psychologist friend of mine is fond of saying, "The unconscious always wins." Her point is to normalize the fact that most human behavior is governed by habit—or unconscious conditioned instinct. The point of this book is to lay out possibilities for behavior governed by conscious intention—to shift as often as possible from the merely habitual to the aware and intentional.

When you do find yourself acting out of habit rather than intentionality, cut yourself some slack. Don't spend any time beating yourself up about whether you're able to be aware and intentional all the time. That would be super human. Instead, enjoy the stretch towards intentionality. As you stretch, consider the Four Disciplines as your allies, not your knuckle-rappers. Let yourself fall in love with their utility as well as their beauty, and let that love pull you along the path they reveal.

Part I

Radical Responsibility and the Four Disciplines

CLARITY
Mind/Mental (air)
Clarity is being curious while discerning.
It elevates the conversation.
Reactive Patterns:
judgment and confusion

INTEGRITY
Body/Physical (earth)
Integrity is being true.
It sustains your life and relationships.
Reactive Patterns:
control and passiveness

Radical Responsibility

INSPIRATION
Spirit/Spiritual (fire)
Inspiration is attuning to your spirit.
It activates meaning and aliveness.
Reactive Patterns:
arrogance and self-deflation

COURAGE
Heart/Emotional (water)
Courage is being wholehearted.
It strengthens emotional presence.
Reactive Patterns:
defensiveness and withdrawal

Warm-up Questions

+ How do I define the word *responsibility*?

+ What does it mean to me to be free?

+ In what ways do I feel powerful in my life? In what ways not?

+ What patterns of thinking and behavior get in the way of me having the life and impact I want to have?

Chapter One

Radical Responsibility

Our deepest fear is not that we are inadequate.
Our deepest fear is that we are powerful beyond measure.
It is our light, not our darkness, that most frightens us.
We ask ourselves, who am I to be brilliant, gorgeous, talented, fabulous?
Actually, who are you not to be?
You are a child of God. Your playing small doesn't serve the world.
There's nothing enlightened about shrinking so that other people won't
feel insecure around you. We are all meant to shine, as children do.
We were born to make manifest the glory of God that is within us.
It's not just in some of us; it's in everyone.
And as we let our own light shine,
we unconsciously give other people permission to do the same.
As we're liberated from our own fear,
our presence automatically liberates others.

Marianne Williamson, *A Return to Love*

I CAN'T KNOW FOR SURE that what you are most afraid of is how powerful you actually are. But I do suspect there are some ways that you "play small" in your life. Some ways that you hold yourself back, or don't fully unleash your real power—in other words, your potential to live an amazing life and have a deeply positive impact in your world.

Every so often I take a day or half-day to be by myself and reflect on my life through journaling and meditation. In one of these mini retreats I was contemplating my relationship with my wife and our commitment to being in relationship in a way that liberates rather than limits each other's growth and fulfillment. As I reflected on how I could be more liberating in my marriage, I reached out silently to Spirit (my word for God) and asked the question, "How can I free her?" Usually when I ask questions like that I get helpful whispers of insight. In this case I got a very loud answer coming back out of the silence. In a strong Irish lilt, I heard a voice in my head say, "Forget about her, free your own fu**ing self."

The Four Disciplines empower you to "free your own... self" to become a more conscious leader—so that, as Williamson says, your presence has a liberating impact on others.

To be in relationship with the Four Disciplines is like showing up each day to apprentice with the masters of a craft—only this is about mastering the craft that is your life and the positive impact you can have on others.

This chapter describes the prerequisites for a rewarding apprenticeship. The first is taking a stance in life of *radical responsibility*. Second is understanding the concept of *discipline* in a very particular way, and as the primary tool of radical responsibility. And third is understanding that within every discipline is the potential for *reactive patterns* to show up as completely normal opportunities to learn and grow.

What Radical Responsibility Is

Former US President Barack Obama, in his first election campaign, popularized the words, "We are the ones we've been waiting for." This notion of *a world waiting* for us points to something that exists in almost everyone—a sense of there being more personal power in ourselves than we have awakened to or are bringing into the world. Occasionally, in a moment of deeper reflection, when you realize how short life is, you may ask yourself what *you* are waiting for. In other words, what's holding you back from all that you're here on the planet to experience and contribute?

The most immediately potent response to that question is actually your willingness—your willingness to wake up and show up, to be more conscious, to be *radically responsible* for your thoughts, feelings, actions, experience, and impact. The term *radical* with responsibility means it's both a *different kind* of responsibility, and a *more rigorous expression* of it.

Radical Responsibility Is Different and More Rigorous

It's not your normal notion of responsibility, which often means shouldering a burden or being to blame for something. Radical responsibility is *different* from that. It is exciting rather than heavy. It may demand a lot from you, but it does not mean that everything is yours to do, that everything is your fault, that you can or should control everything, or that every time there's a screw up you should punish yourself or blame someone else.

What it does mean is that you jump in with all of your devotion and capabilities ablaze. This is the *more rigorous* part. Whatever your life is devoted to—whether it's success in business, raising a family, or expressing yourself artistically—radical responsibility is a fierce commitment to contribute, rather than a weighty obligation. When you read this, you may be tempted to think that radical responsibility means it's your job to save the world—whether your team, or your friends or children. It's not. It's simply your job to love the world.

Radical Responsibility Is Presence— Awareness and Intentionality

In loving your world, you are most fundamentally responsible for your presence in it—for showing up in life remembering each moment is a precious gift to be *present to*, and a cherished opportunity to be *present in*.

Imagine, for example, sitting with a group of people having a conversation. It could be a business team, a group of friends, your family, a school parents committee, you name it. With your *awareness*, you are *present to* yourself and the conversation, and with your *intentionality*, you are *present in* it.

Awareness is open, receptive, and available to your own thoughts and feelings, as well as to what is happening around you (people, Nature, conversations, events, trends, challenges, opportunities, etc).

Intentionality is consciously choosing the way you bring yourself into whatever conversation or situation you're in. It's about showing up wherever you are with the potency of who you are.

Radical Responsibility Is Life-Affirming

You and all human beings are meant to be present—to be aware and intentional—in the world in a way that honors Life. In a way that is not neutral, but that makes a positive difference in your own experience, and in the quality of life around you. Rather than merely taking up space, you are born to be a *life-affirming presence on the planet*.

To be evolving as a life-affirming presence is a defining quality of radical responsibility. Not as a prescription for who or how you should be, but rather a calling—an invitation to keep reflecting on and choosing what it means for you in any moment to show up in a way that is life affirming.

When you do that—when you ask yourself what is life-affirming in any moment, and you commit to defining and refining what that means for you—you are on the path of awakening and activating what it means to be fully responsible for your presence.

Radical Responsibility Is Your Power to Create

Radical responsibility is taking seriously your power to create your life and your world. *"Be the change you want to see in the world,"* Gandhi is reported to have said. To be radically responsible is to look inside yourself for the cause of what you see in your world, not to find blame, but to find personal power. You imagine the kind of world you want to live in and ask yourself whether you are being the kind of person that creates that world.

You reflect on questions like: If I see bigotry in the world, what part of me is a bigot? If I see violence and abuse, what part of me is violent and abusive or does not stand up to bullies? If I see complacency or mediocrity, what part of me is not committed to excellence?

You have countless opportunities to be a creative force in your world each day—in emails, conversations, car rides, big and small interactions and decisions. Whatever you are up to, consider the kind of world you want to live in and help create, and be and do what that world calls for.

Radical Responsibility Is Choosing to Respond

When you are radically responsible, you know that within the events, circumstances and relationships of your life and profession—many of which will be extremely challenging—you are 100% responsible for your choices. It means that you always have choice, even when it doesn't seem that way. You claim as a privilege (not shoulder as a burden) your *response-ability*—your *ability to respond*—from your own best internal impulses and highest wisdom. You empower yourself to choose how to respond to relationships, circumstances, and events.

This kind of responsibility liberates you. How much time and energy gets tied up and wasted on stuff you can't control—when you're wishing that someone else would act differently, or that some circumstance was different than it is? Instead, radical responsibility invites you to engage in *repeated acts of liberation* by focusing on what you can influence and letting go of the rest.

PARADIGM SHIFT ALERT
From: Responsibility means shouldering burdens or taking blame.
To: Responsibility means the privilege and liberation of claiming your *ability to respond*—your ability to choose.

Radical Responsibility Is the Ground of Transformation

When you put radical responsibility at the center of your life, you become a change agent. Not because you are trying to change things, or even trying to change yourself, but because you are creating the conditions through your presence—through your awareness and intentionality—for transformation to occur.

With radical responsibility, transformation arises from inner discipline that creates the conditions for outer change to occur. Your focus becomes less about *driving* change, and more about creating the conditions for change to occur by focusing on the kind of person you are. There is the potential for change all around you all the time. If there's one thing we can really trust about life—and this is part of what *a sacred trust* means—it's that life changes and evolves. Built into life, into all our relationships, and into all our business initiatives, is a natural drive toward evolution. Your radical responsibility—your focus on awareness, intention, and choice about how to act—is how you participate in life's natural drive to evolve through transformation.

The Way of Discipline

From time to time, I make a big collage (using words and photos from magazines) known as a vision board to remind myself of my personal vision. For one of these boards I pulled the words from a magazine ad, "Solid. Disciplined. Thorough. And other titillating adjectives."

That line disrupts the common notion of discipline. Because for most people, the word "discipline" conjures up a not-so-sexy combination of stoicism, self-denial, duty, punishment, and cracking the whip on ourselves.

While it may be a little over the top to think of discipline as "titillating," we can stop thinking of it as stoic obligation. Instead, we can conjure up inspiring images like Socrates sitting in dialogue with his students, an Aikido master in the flow of a precise action, or Serena Williams' smashing forehand.

The word discipline comes from "disciple"—an earnest student of a topic worthy of devotion. Modern-day disciplines range from an academic field of study, to medicine, to science, to marketing, to a yoga practice. Discipline as *discipleship* takes on a quality of devotion, and a commitment to excellence. It replaces external sticks and carrots with innate drive and passion.

The Four Disciplines are just that—disciplines—that when practiced together from a mindset of radical responsibility, activate *conscious leadership*. Coming back to Serena Williams, imagine the millions of times Serena has practiced each element of her game. Her forehand is a discipline. So is her backhand, her serve, her volley, and her mental and emotional state. All are disciplines, that when combined together on the court, activate the brilliance that is Serena's game.

The Four Disciplines work like that—like a champion's tennis game. While they are individual disciplines, as an integrated whole they are more powerful than the sum of the parts. As you more naturally live each discipline through practice, they combine to form your complete inner game, enabling you to show up in the world with more life-affirming presence, brilliance, and power.

Fierce Love

For something to be a true discipline, doing it can't feel like drudgery, or your practice of it will never take hold and never last. There needs to be a passion behind it. There needs to be your love behind it. Contemplate discipline as *fierce love in action*. It is loving the world enough to follow through on your best intentions. It is loving yourself enough to take the lid off what is great and worthy inside you. It is the kind of love that liberates—that frees up your energy for its best use. It is not namby-pamby love. It is fierce, fire-in-the-eyes love.

When you think you need to be more disciplined, connect with what you fiercely love. Let what you deeply care about drive you. Consider the role of discipline in your life not as your slave-driver, but as your liberator.

That kind of liberating discipline—as fierce love—makes your presence more powerful and compelling for the people who enter into it. Fierce love also brings you into more powerful presence with yourself. When you look at yourself through the eyes of fierce love, you see all of who you are—the ugly along with the noble and beautiful—and with compassion, you invite yourself to shed those characteristics, mindsets and behaviors that limit you.

PARADIGM SHIFT ALERT
From: Discipline is you cracking the whip on yourself.
To: Discipline is fiercely loving yourself and your world enough to devote yourself to the things that are most important to you.

A State of Being

The Four Disciplines are not things you have, like having Courage or having Integrity. They are states of being that you apprentice yourself to.

Discipline is a type of intense attention, with its primary focus on the kind of person you are *being*.

Imagine concentric circles. The inner circle is labeled *being*, outside that circle is *doing*, and then *having*. It's the reverse of what most of us are taught—which is to define ourselves first by what we have, then what we do, and then last, if at all, by *who we are*. But what if you lived the other way around—starting first with who you are—in other words, your way of *being*. What if you knew that who you are is the source of what you do, and what you have?

We are too rarely taught this in our schools or families. We are taught primarily how to achieve things—how to get recognition, good grades, money, romantic attention. And we are taught, even if not explicitly, that this is power. If we are taught anything about how to be, it's a sidebar, an adjunct to our doing and achieving. And hardly anyone refers to your being as your power.

To focus on your being—on who you are—means that rather than thinking about how to get love, you are thinking about how to be loving. Instead of trying to get rewarded, your attention is on contribution. Rather than trying to get belonging (acceptance by others), your focus is on being someone who belongs, someone who can include yourself.

As you focus on the qualities of your *being*, your *doing* becomes increasingly more authentic and effective, and your *having* becomes more satisfying.

To elevate the quality of your being requires ongoing reflection and self-awareness. I often work with executive clients in a one-day or two-day immersive format. It's a way of going deep enough to create real transformation. For many leaders, it's the first time in their lives they've had an experience of this kind. In talking with the CEO of a large global company a few weeks after his immersion, I asked him what insights he had that were making the biggest difference in the way he was leading. After sharing a couple of the most significant ones, he said, "You know, one of the biggest changes is simply being more reflective." This is a man who had spent the last 35 years very successfully building his career and his business acumen. His words were a reminder to me of how rare it actually is for leaders to take time out from busily doing, even for short moments, to deeply reflect on who they are choosing to *be*.

Reactive Patterns

If discipline is a kind of fiercely loving self-empowerment, enabling us to be conscious and intentional about the lives and impact we are creating, reactive patterns are the opposite—arising from insecurity, anxiety, and fear, tending to sabotage our best intentions.

Being reactive is the opposite of exercising your creative power. It dis-empowers you. In relation to the Four Disciplines, reactive patterns show up as a distortion of the Discipline on one hand, or a repression of the Discipline on the other.

A distortion is an attempt to be powerful in the world—but instead of enabling genuine personal power, as the Discipline does, a distortion takes away from your power.

A repression, on the other hand, is an abdication of your power, running directly counter to the Discipline.

For example, take the first of the Four Disciplines—Inspiration. The distortion of Inspiration is *arrogance*. Consider the possibility that arrogance does not generally come with mal-intent, but rather is an attempt—albeit a distorted one—to be inspired. Inspiration is, in its essence, your connection to Spirit. Arrogance is a kind of persona-driven façade of that connection.

On the other hand, the repression of Inspiration—which can be just as debilitating, and sometimes even more limiting than arrogance—is self-deflation. Self-deflation is also a denial of your authentic connection to Spirit.

Reactive patterns tend to crop up when you feel under threat or stress—whether chronic or in-the-moment. You will see how this is true as you study the specific distortions and repressions in each of the Four Disciplines.

Identifying the reactive patterns—the distortions and repressions—that oppose each Discipline, and seeing how and why they operate, helps the Disciplines stand out in contrast. Seeing how reactivity limits you opens a backdoor to understanding how the Disciplines empower you.

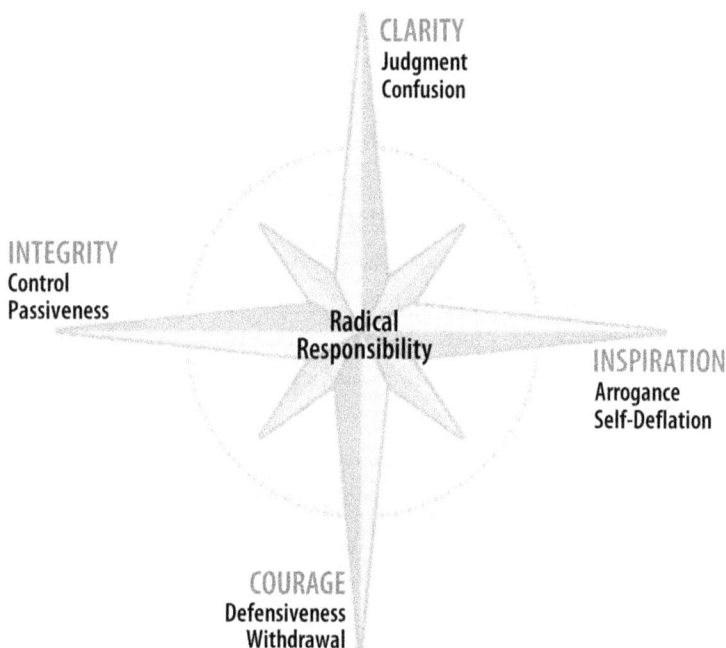

```
                    CLARITY
                    Judgment
                    Confusion



INTEGRITY
Control
Passiveness              Radical
                         Responsibility
                                           INSPIRATION
                                           Arrogance
                                           Self-Deflation




            COURAGE
            Defensiveness
            Withdrawal
```

Reactive Patterns—in distorted and repressed forms—
exist in contrast to each Discipline.

A Story of Two Wolves

A young Native American boy and his grandfather are sitting by the fire, and the boy is deep in thought. "Grandson," says the grandfather, "you look troubled. Why is your heart heavy?"

"Because Grandfather," the boy says, "There are two wolves inside me, and they are fighting. One is full of judgment, blame, lies, anger, laziness and arrogance. The other is generous, loving, truthful, humble, and courageous. Grandfather, please tell me which wolf will win."

The elder looks away, takes a puff on his pipe, and says, "Grandson, the wolf that will win is the wolf you feed."

The Four Disciplines feed your authentic power to create your life and the quality of your impact. This authentic power, honoring leadership as a sacred trust, is your *Creative Wolf*. The opposite of your authentic power—the opposite of radical responsibility—is reactivity. This is your *Reactive Wolf*.

Reactivity is the exact opposite of responsibility and discipline. What's ironic is that reactivity can look like responsibility because it is generated by an immature, unconscious part of yourself as a way to feel secure and powerful.

The price for this kind of false security and imitation power is a loss of freedom and actual personal power. You get trapped in habit. Reactive means you re-act. In other words, your behavior follows a habitual pattern that got created at an early point in your life as a strategy to keep you safe, or to get love and validation. A reactive pattern, instead of being driven by your highest values, purpose, mental and emotional intelligence, and wisdom, is driven by your fear. It does not create what you truly want, but more likely either a façade of what you want, or a very watered-down version of it.

It is important to remember, and have compassion for the fact, that reactive patterns live in each of us. We all react. It's neurologically wired in us. It's human. We have both wolves in us. While we are wired to creatively evolve, ironically we're also wired for reactivity. Both are natural states. In the early days of human existence, we depended on our reactivity for survival. It's what kept us out of the tiger's jaws. The "flight or fight" reptilian brain was essential. While not as essential these days, our fear comes in handy when there's real danger. Knowing the difference between a *healthy intuitive sense of danger*, and an *unhealthy fearful stance in life*, is the key.

From Reactive to Creative

Creative discipline or reactivity—you choose which wolf to feed—the Creative Wolf, or the Reactive Wolf. How do you choose responsibility and discipline over reactivity, moment by moment? How do you bring the Creative Wolf forward, especially in the middle of a frustrating meeting or an argument with your spouse?

> *Between stimulus and response there is a space. In that space is our power to choose our response. In our response lies our growth and our freedom.*
>
> Viktor Frankl, Holocaust survivor, psychologist,
> and author of *Man's Search for Meaning*

Calling on your *Creative Wolf*, while not always easy to do, is conceptually simple. It involves creating a *space* between *stimulus*—whether an event, an interaction, a triggering moment, or a choice to make—and *reaction*. As you start to recognize these moments of opportunity, you can then practice choosing something different. You can override the *reaction* with a *creative response*. At times, this may seem impossible. But the more resourced you are—getting enough sleep, meditating and reflecting, having positive experiences, feeling nourished at all levels—the more easily you will be able to choose a creative response versus reacting. Also, the more you generate conscious awareness of the mindsets and behaviors you want to show up—through the Four Disciplines—the more available those ways of being are to you in that space between stimulus and response.

To move from reactivity to creative response, ask yourself, "Is this what I always do?" And if it is, "Is it creating the life and impact I want to have?" If it's not creating what you want, ask yourself what you could do instead.

Every time you create a space between stimulus and reaction, and override the reaction with a more creative response, you lay down new patterns in your whole-body neurological system. The Four Disciplines lay out a blueprint for those patterns. Practicing them feeds the *Creative Wolf* in you, reminding you of your best self, and empowering you to live from that best self.

Self-Compassion

Because no one can be powerfully and creatively engaged in life all the time, the discipline of radical responsibility must include compassion for where you are on your journey, and where you are on any given day. It's not being lazy with where you are, but also not berating yourself for the ways you fall short. Your self-compassion, rather than letting yourself off the hook, ironically makes you more available to contribute because you aren't having to defend yourself against your own internal criticism. You can stay open and connected to a kind of *no-kidding* urgency to be acutely aware of your world, and intentional about how you show up in it.

Chapter 1 Summary Points

The world needs you; the stakes are high; and, it's a choice—not an obligation—to live as if your life and relationship with your world is sacred and entrusted to you. Which means honoring who you are and who you can be, and taking your personal power and impact earnestly.

To choose life and leadership as a sacred trust requires letting go of old ways of being that limit you and keep you small. It means not fearing your own power, but claiming it as a gift.

What Radical Responsibility Is

Radical responsibility is the core mindset for leading a life of greater personal power and effectiveness. It is being fully aware of and intentional about your experience of life, and your impact. It requires a simultaneous connection to yourself and attention to your world. It engages your power to choose. It demands that you *be the change you want to see in the world.*

Radical responsibility is most empowering when you see it as liberation, rather than burden; and less about saving the world, and more about loving it—including compassion for yourself when you fall short of your best.

The Way of Discipline

Being disciplined is being devoted to something—whether it's a field of study or a quality of being you want to embody. Your life will always reflect the degree of discipline you bring to it. Discipline, when it is devotion to something worthwhile, is a kind of fierce love for yourself, and for your world. When you choose fierce love over being your own slave driver, you liberate energy for change.

Reactive Patterns
Reactivity is the opposite of exercising radical responsibility through the Disciplines. Being able to observe your reactive patterns—tending toward either distortion or repression—helps you recommit and recalibrate to the corresponding Disciplines.

Chapter 1 Journaling
What speaks to me most powerfully in the quote from Marianne Williamson is...

What makes sense to me about radical responsibility is...
What I find challenging about radical responsibility is...

When I'm trying to make a change or accomplish a goal, if I thought of discipline as fierce love (versus forcing myself to do something), the difference it would make in my life experience would be...

Some strategies I already use to feed my Creative Wolf are...

What triggers my Reactive Wolf is...
The learning I take from that is...

Warm-up Questions

- What does "human nature" mean to me?

- When do I feel most inspired and energized in my life?

- What does it mean to me to be "in integrity," and "out of integrity?"

- In what ways am I courageous, and in what ways not?

- On the spectrum of judging others on one hand to being curious about them on the other, where do I tend to be?

The Four Disciplines Blueprint

RADICAL RESPONSIBILITY puts you square in the center of yourself. It is an awareness that by and large you are the cause in your life.

From this place in yourself—we'll call it your command center—you are well positioned to fully harness the gifts of the Four Disciplines. Let's start to unwrap those gifts by exploring with a broad brush what the Disciplines are and what potential they hold for your life and leadership.

Building on the Elements of Human Nature Design

Imagine building a home with no design as a blueprint to build from. This is how most people build their lives—without an intentionally chosen framework to orient themselves to. Even if you are extremely goal-driven and efficient in getting things done, you may not have consciously chosen a coherent internal blueprint to guide you on your journey through life.

A blueprint organizes and focuses your attention. It gives you a place to point your awareness, and a system for asking yourself the questions that will make your life more enjoyable and impactful. Questions like: Are you inspired much of the time? Are you aware of when you're judging others, and making assumptions about their actions? Are you being courageous in business meetings, or in conversations with your loved ones? Are you being true to what you believe in, and to what you say you're going to do? These are the types of questions that guide your attention, and your power, as you apprentice to the Four Disciplines. Each Discipline is your teacher, and as you spend more time with it you are like an apprentice with a master, gaining mastery in how you lead your life.

You have many options for blueprints to guide you in your life. Consider the power and authenticity of using your deepest human nature as the blueprint for how you show up as a leader. The Four-Discipline blueprint mirrors the fundamental design of Nature—in its four core elements of fire, earth, water, and air—and thus the fundamental design of the human being as an expression of Nature.

These four core elements make up everything in our physical world. This is obvious with earth, water, and air. If you're wondering about fire, picture the sun. The sun is the ultimate fire—the source of all energy in the biosphere. It would be a cold, lifeless planet without it. The fire burning in your fireplace, or on your gas stove, or in the electric power plant down the road, or that fuels your body, is only available because of the stored solar energy in wood, gas, coal, oil, and the food you eat. The solar fire does more than warm your face. It burns inside you as the ultimate source of energy and heat for your life.

Each Discipline carries the energy of one of these four core elements. A good way to start building a relationship with each Discipline is to develop a curiosity about—and a relationship with—its elemental ground. In other words, what does it feel like to be fiery, earthy, watery, or airy? Notice the presence of these elements in your world—from a mountain stream, to a clear blue sky, to rock formations, to a sunset. What kinds of metaphors do you see?

These fundamental elements of Nature—fire, earth, water, and air—correspond to the domains of life we are most familiar with in ourselves—the spiritual, physical, emotional, and mental.

The Four Disciplines—Inspiration, Integrity, Courage, and Clarity—are the most direct and full ways I have discovered to honor the presence of these fundamental elements of Human Nature in each of us. The Disciplines create a bridge between our most fundamental nature as human beings and the qualities that empower us to effectively lead our lives.

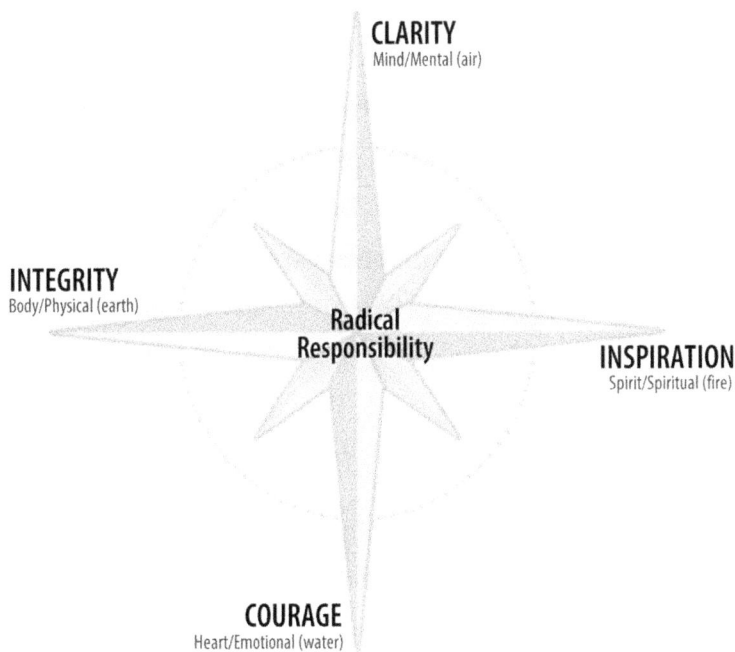

CLARITY
Mind/Mental (air)

INTEGRITY
Body/Physical (earth)

**Radical
Responsibility**

INSPIRATION
Spirit/Spiritual (fire)

COURAGE
Heart/Emotional (water)

The Four Disciplines and the Four Elements

Living our lives in accord with the qualities of our true nature is not a new idea, but it is unusual as a conscious practice to devote yourself to. Most of us have created a persona to live from. Our persona is the face we present to the world as the person we want others to think we are. We present that face, or mask, sometimes intentionally, but most of the time subconsciously (in other words, we don't know we're doing it).

Moving from persona to qualities of being means that every day, and every moment, is an opportunity to spend less energy maintaining a persona and devote more energy to expressing the qualities of your fundamental nature—qualities that enhance your authentic power in the world.

The Discipline of Inspiration

Imagine standing in the center of a giant compass laid out on the ground. You turn to the east, where the sun rises. You feel the sun's warmth on your face. It is radiant and enlivening. This is the place of Inspiration.

It is no coincidence that people from many different cultures around the world have worshiped the sun, and that religious traditions talk about God, or Spirit, in terms of *the Light*. It is also no coincidence that at the time of awakening from a night's sleep to the physical light of the dawn, millions of people orient themselves to the metaphorical light—to their sense of the spiritual, whether they meditate, pray, or quietly reflect on the miracle of Life over a cup of coffee.

Inspiration is your relationship to your light, your fire, your individual spirit. It is also your relationship to *the* Light, and to Spirit with a capital S, as the all-pervasive animating Life-Force of the Universe, and a potential source of sustenance and wisdom in your life. To apprentice yourself to the discipline of Inspiration is to turn your individual spirit toward the sources that feed it—whatever fuels depth and meaning in your life and gives you a sense of being *on fire*.

What Inspiration is: attuning to your spirit
What Inspiration does: activates meaning and aliveness
Reactive Patterns: arrogance and self-deflation

Recall what it's like when your spirit feels dampened, deadened, or even crushed. Inspiration is the opposite of that!

Inspiration as a discipline is about embodying the vibrancy of Life. It is honoring the way Life beckons you to be *on fire*, and to let the light and warmth of your spirit be seen and felt by others.

The essence of Inspiration is claiming your connection to the Life-Force that animates the Universe, and knowing that you can reach inside yourself for this connection in any moment.

Inspiration is making yourself available to the creative fire of Life, and what that creative fire calls forth in you. It is an ongoing act of surrender. Not the kind of surrender that means *giving up*, but rather *giving yourself to* Life. It means embracing and surrendering to the mystery of Life's creative power and devoting yourself to discovering and embodying your particular expression of that power.

Reactive Patterns Limiting Inspiration

Arrogance—Inspiration is an ongoing process of nourishing your spirit, being connected to your unique values and purpose, and cultivating your aliveness. The distortion of Inspiration is arrogance. Arrogance is *separation from your spirit*—which usually stems from getting too enamored with your own persona—its image, success, and failure. In arrogance, being Spirit-centered is distorted into being persona-centered.

Self-Deflation—The repressed version of Inspiration is self-deflation—which like arrogance is also a separation from Spirit. When you deflate yourself, you deny the spiritual inheritance of your own brilliance and beauty. You abdicate the power in your spiritual nature.

Arrogance and Self-Deflation:

* separate you from potential sources of real meaning in your life.

* indicate a lack of true confidence, and a dependence on external sources of validation.

* make you less available to meaningful connection with others by making what you have to offer them less substantial and

less authentic, as well as limiting your ability to see and experience what others have to offer to you.

◆ create an energetic drain on relationships—both professional and personal.

PARADIGM SHIFT ALERT
From: Self-deflation is humility.
To: Self-deflation is the opposite of true humility.
Instead of devotion to a Life-Force and purpose larger than yourself—which is true humility—self-deflation is rejecting the unique gifts of your spiritual inheritance.

The Discipline of Integrity

Integrity sits across from Inspiration on the Four Disciplines Medicine Wheel. Imagine literally standing inside the wheel marked out on the ground as a giant compass. You've been facing the east—the place of Inspiration. You turn your body and attention 180 degrees to the west—the place of Integrity. In that movement, you get a sense of the way that most worthwhile endeavors in life are fundamentally an interplay of inspiration and integrity—a way of honoring the intangible values and ideals we cherish by living them in tangible ways.

While Inspiration is connection to what has meaning, Integrity is being true to that connection. It calls you to translate your passions and dreams into the actions that create your experience and influence your world.

What Integrity is: being true

What Integrity does: sustains your life and relationships

Reactive Patterns: control and passiveness

The shorthand for Integrity is *being true*. Integrity holds the grounded energy of being true to yourself and others, and delivering on what creates both physical well-being and traction in your life, which means:

- Being honest, especially with yourself, about what you see as true—in yourself and in your world.

- Aligning your words and actions with your most noble self, and your highest sense of what creates meaning, wholeness, and balance in your life.

- Holding true to high standards of excellence.

- Standing up for, and following through on, what you believe in.

- Taking care of your physical world, especially your own body.

When you want to make a bicycle wheel perfectly round, you "true" the wheel. Truing the wheel aligns it with its purpose of rolling smoothly over the pavement. This is how integrity works. Integrity aligns you with your most cherished values, with what's good and noble about you, and with your standards of excellence for yourself.

Integrity is what holds things together. It's because of integrity that there are things we can count on. Your house standing up. Contracts working. Your marriage commitment being honored. Your doctor being in the office when you have an appointment. Your paycheck showing up in your bank account.

Integrity is being true to ourselves, each other, our sense of excellence, and the well-being of our own bodies, not because we "should," but because it sets us free. To be true is liberating, rather than confining. While you may be tempted to think of Integrity as something that boxes you in, consider the idea that it in fact liberates you from the pretense of trying to be someone you're not, and from the diminishing impact of saying or doing things that are not aligned with your highest ideals and interests.

Over the years, I have worked with leaders who have struggled with various types of personal problems, including addiction. When one particular client thoroughly got hold of the notion of Integrity as liberating, he found the breakthrough he was looking for in kicking his cocaine addiction. He knew that his addiction was keeping him from fully living the inspired life he was capable of. When he saw that integrity—aligning with his highest self—actually liberated him, rather than acting as a kill-joy, that shift in mindset gave him the strength to change his behavior.

PARADIGM SHIFT ALERT
From: Integrity is a confining kill-joy.
To: Integrity liberates you to experience true joy and fulfillment in life.

Reactive Patterns Limiting Integrity

Control—The distortion of Integrity is control. Integrity is about alignment, not control—about actively aligning with who you are and what fuels meaning and aliveness in your life, so that the outcomes you want flow naturally from that alignment. It is being true to your promises to Life, to yourself, and to others. It is uprightness, like having a strong flexible backbone.

It may seem like a subtle difference, but it's an important one—recognizing that Integrity is being in alignment with yourself, rather than in control of your world or the circumstances of your life. This is a fairly radical stance because it means being true to your best self and letting the chips fall as they may, rather than lose your Integrity in an effort to control the world around you. The game of trying to control things outside yourself is a distortion of actual Integrity. It shows up as rigidity, micromanagement, being too rule-bound; and in the extreme, bullying and/or being obsessive/compulsive.

Passiveness—Integrity when repressed is a kind of spinelessness and inaction. You don't follow through on your intentions. You take your eye off the ball and leave it for others to pick up and carry. You are inattentive to all that holds your physical world together. You fail to act in ways that create traction.

Metaphorically, Integrity is a warm firm handshake. Control is a vice-grip, and passiveness is a limp-fish handshake.

PARADIGM SHIFT ALERT
From: People who are controlling are intentionally being bossy, bullying, or perfectionistic.
To: People who are controlling are most likely well-intentioned, coming from a place of attempting to be in integrity, but overdoing it because they feel insecure or anxious.

Control and Passiveness:

• disempower and demotivate people (teams, families, spouses)—through micromanagement and impossibly-high standards, or often double standards; or through inattention, lower standards and expectations, and a lack of accountability.

- can create a toxic and even abusive environment—through perfectionism or bullying; or by allowing injustice by not standing up to it.

- erode credibility, generate resistance and resentment, and discourage constructive conversations and collaboration.

The Discipline of Courage

The word courage evolved from Latin (cor) to French (corage) to Middle English (courage), always meaning "of the heart." "Take heart" means "be courageous." To be "disheartened" means your courage is failing.

Typically though, when we're talking about the heart, we mean something like compassion or loving connection. And we mostly associate courage with bravery rather than things of the heart. As one of the Four Disciplines, however, Courage includes all of the above—bravery, compassion, love and appreciation—and more. Courage is your willingness to experience the whole spectrum of emotions (including the difficult ones) that create intimacy with life, and make life a wholehearted adventure.

What Courage is: being wholehearted
What Courage does: strengthens emotional presence
Reactive Patterns: defensiveness and withdrawal

Every so often, when I feel the need to deepen my intimacy with Life, I go off into the mountains or woods to be alone. One such adventure took me to the northern Minnesota wilderness for a 20-day solo vision quest. About half-way into the 20 days, I found myself on an island, where I was enjoying a very quiet, uneventful day, mostly sitting, sometimes reading. Suddenly, what sounded like flying castanets shattered the silence. I followed the noise to a fat tree stump. What I saw was intense—a large blue dragonfly eating a smaller one alive. And as I watched, a line from a book of wisdom I had been reading a moment before struck me like a lightning bolt: "Say yes to life," it read, "even though you know it will devour you."

This is being wholehearted—saying yes to life even though you know it brings loss and pain, just as it brings beauty and magic. Being wholehearted, versus half-hearted, is risky and courageous. When you show up wholehearted, you're all in. You put yourself on the line. You're available to experience all the emotions evoked by the richness of life and relationship.

Courage is *seeking into* life, meaning opening yourself to all of life, not just the parts that are nice. It's the opposite of stoicism, playing it safe, and shrinking or pulling back from life. It is playing full-out and leaning into life with a sense of adventure.

You can tell when Courage falls off and fear takes over. Take a sports team for example. It's obvious when a sports team stops playing to win, and starts playing *not to lose*. Their energy changes. They get cautious and tight. The game is no longer an adventure. It's a series of calculated risks. It may even look like their hearts are no longer in the game. The truth is, they're not. Their hearts and sense of adventure have checked out.

To live wholeheartedly means you don't run scared. But that requires some ground of trust underneath your feet. Many believe this ground of trust comes from outside themselves. They're waiting for the people they can trust, or the circumstances they can trust. But trust doesn't come *from* the reliability of your world, and the people in it. It comes from knowing you can rely on yourself to stay true to yourself *in* your world, and *with* the people in it. From that inner reliability, you show up in the circumstances and relationships of your life. From that strength of heart, and the ground of safety it creates, you can venture outside your comfort zone, from a mindset of trusting in yourself to create a ground of safety wherever you are.

PARADIGM SHIFT ALERT
From: Living with a sense of trust comes from knowing that your world and the people in it are reliable.
To: Living with a sense of trust comes from knowing that you can rely on yourself to be true to yourself as you interact with your world and the people in it.

Reactive Patterns Limiting Courage

Defensiveness—Courage is your heart open to life, even when you're afraid or hurt. Defensiveness—the distorted version of Courage—is reacting to pain, or to feeling threatened or offended, by closing your heart and making it less available. It's an attempt to avoid the discomfort of emotions you don't want to feel—hurt, sadness, insecurity, or at times even positive emotions like joy.

Defensiveness is very instinctual, arising from a feeling of getting backed into a corner, where your persona thinks the only thing you can do is lash out in defense. Rather than being informed by uncomfortable emotion, you let the bad feeling take control. Because defensiveness has an aggressive energy, it can look like Courage. It can look like bravely protecting your values or your boundaries. But in actuality, it is a distortion of Courage, protecting yourself from facing the difficult emotions evoked by other people or the events and circumstances of your life.

Withdrawal—The repression of Courage is withdrawal. In the face of difficult emotion, withdrawal is shrinking away, avoiding, or denying. Like when you're faced with someone else's anger and you emotionally walk away instead of staying in connection and working out the issue with them.

When you consider both defensiveness and withdrawal, you may recognize that you tend toward one or the other when you react, rather than respond, to the events, circumstances, and interactions in life that are hard on your heart. And, it may be that whether you retreat or numb out in the face of discomfort, or you lash out at people defensively, depends on who or what you're facing. You may default to one strategy with your spouse and another with your boss—often reflecting the power dynamics of the particular relationship.

Defensiveness and Withdrawal:

- stop the processes of learning and creative thinking because the fight or flight mechanism shuts down the learning centers of the brain.

- hurt relationships and trust, impeding the flow of information and collaboration.

- escalate aggression (including passive aggression), cutting off emotional availability and empathy.

- perpetuate a victim mentality.

The Discipline of Clarity

Most people think of clarity as knowing something for sure. But the discipline of Clarity is less about holding a rigid point of view, and more about being mentally spacious. In other words, you're willing and able to make space in yourself for both intense curiosity and firm conviction, both open-mindedness and discernment.

What Clarity is: being curious while discerning
What Clarity does: elevates the conversation
Reactive Patterns: judgment and confusion

Clarity is showing up in the arena of ideas and conversation in a way that is very different from holding rigid positions of right and wrong. You can't meet yourself or anyone else in a place of Clarity if you hold on too tightly to your points of view, or label as wrong other ways of thinking, or if you aren't curious, open, and relating from a mindset of respect.

PARADIGM SHIFT ALERT
From: Clarity is being certain of the right answer or solution.
To: Clarity is being curious and open-minded, while also being willing to choose a point of view.

Even when you really do think someone else is wrong, you can decide to see their perspective not as wrong, but simply as one that *you* don't choose. You may even vehemently not share their perspective. That's fine. The point is to give yourself permission to have your own point of view without making someone else wrong. In a sense, making them wrong invalidates their perspective, rather than making it something to add to the mix of information you are open to considering.

Being curiously open to a wide range of information is half the Clarity story. The other half is choosing a strong point of view. While these aspects of Clarity might seem opposed, they are actually powerful complements to each other. The synergy of openness and discernment enables you to see the range of choices, the ambiguities, the unknowns, the paradoxes—and out of all that, arrive at insights, learning, decisions, and strategies.

Clarity as a discipline is as much about your thinking *process* (staying curious and open) as it is about the *outcomes* (understanding, knowing, decision, conviction) of your thinking.

Being both open and discerning elevates all your conversations—whether in your own head, or with others—enabling those conversations to be more creative, generating more of the experience you want, and impact you intend.

Reactive Patterns Limiting Clarity

Judgment—Clarity is being both open-minded and discerning—a paradoxical combination that combines both curiosity about the world and conviction in your point of view. When the power of Clarity is distorted, it looks more like closed-minded judgment. This sounds like "I'm right, you're wrong," and often "I'm good, you're bad."

Confusion—The repression of Clarity is confusion. It sounds like "I don't know what to think." Confusion as we're using the term here is not lack of understanding. It's an unwillingness to choose a point of view, chart a course, or make a decision.

In judgment, you blame, criticize, and write people and ideas off as bad or wrong. In Clarity, you get curious about the value in any perspective.

In confusion, you abandon discernment. In Clarity, you explore, learn and choose a point of view.

Judgment and Confusion:

- shut down constructive dialogue because points of view are too fixed or too nebulous.

- make your conversation too limited, or too open-ended.

- create disconnection and mistrust and limit creative collaboration.

- Justify hate and violence—in their subtle and not-so-subtle forms.

- create rifts in teams, families, marriages, communities and among countries.

Chapter 2 Summary Points

Building on the Elements of Human Nature Design

If your intent is to become a more authentically powerful human being and leader, it helps to have a framework of consciousness to operate from. When that blueprint is built on the fundamental elements of human nature, it empowers you from your very core.

The elements of fire, earth, water, and air are the forces of Nature that give rise to the human dimensions of the spiritual, physical, emotional, and mental—and empower you as a force of Nature. The disciplines of Inspiration, Integrity, Courage, and Clarity are built on the forces of Human Nature. Embracing these Disciplines is an empowering alternative to projecting a persona to the world.

The Discipline of Inspiration

Inspiration is the discipline of being connected to Spirit. It sustains your passion. It is honoring the guidance of your own spirit and the larger creative force that animates all life.

There is a confidence and a spiritual self-authority and nobility in Inspiration. The distortion, or façade, of that confidence is arrogance. Or, when Inspiration is repressed, it is self-deflation.

The Discipline of Integrity

Integrity is the discipline of honesty and honoring. It supports authentic action. It is being grounded in what's true. It is attention and devotion to what it takes to keep things real, and to make things tangible in the world.

Integrity has a quality of backbone, impeccability, excellence, and dedication to the quality of your physical existence. When the healthy impulse of Integrity to be true and aligned is distorted, it becomes control, which can look like perfectionism or bullying in relationship. Inspiration repressed is Inaction, which limits your power to manifest what you want in your life and relationships.

The Discipline of Courage

Courage is the discipline of being wholehearted. It strengthens your emotional presence. Being wholehearted doesn't mean that your heart never gets hurt, but that it stays in the game even when it's painful. Being wholehearted is honoring the emotional dimension of life, embracing emotions as a source of both information and richness.

Courage chooses love over fear—being willing to throw your whole heart into life, relationship, and leadership—knowing you risk failure and disappointment.

The distortion of true Courage is defensiveness, and its repressed version is withdrawal. Defensiveness and withdrawal are akin to *fight or flight*.

The Discipline of Clarity

Clarity is the discipline of being responsible for your thoughts and language in a way that empowers you and others, elevating all your conversations. Clarity is intentionally using your mind to create the quality of your experience. It employs the paradoxical notion of being curious and open to perspectives while at the same time being incisively discerning among them.

The distortion of Clarity is judgment. Repressed Clarity is confusion, which is being unable or unwilling to take a point of view.

CLARITY
Mind/Mental (air)
Clarity is being curious while discerning.
It elevates the conversation.
Reactive Patterns:
judgment and confusion

INTEGRITY
Body/Physical (earth)
Integrity is being true.
It sustains your life and relationships.
Reactive Patterns:
control and passiveness

Radical Responsibility

INSPIRATION
Spirit/Spiritual (fire)
Inspiration is attuning to your spirit.
It activates meaning and aliveness.
Reactive Patterns:
arrogance and self-deflation

COURAGE
Heart/Emotional (water)
Courage is being wholehearted.
It strengthens emotional presence.
Reactive Patterns:
defensiveness and withdrawal

Chapter 2 Journaling

The Discipline I am most intrigued by is...

The Discipline I naturally have the **most** well-developed relationship with is....

The Discipline I naturally have the **least** well-developed relationship with is....

The reactive patterns (distortions and repressions) I tend to fall into most are...

The ways these qualities impact my life and leadership are...

Part II

The Core Practices
of the Four Disciplines

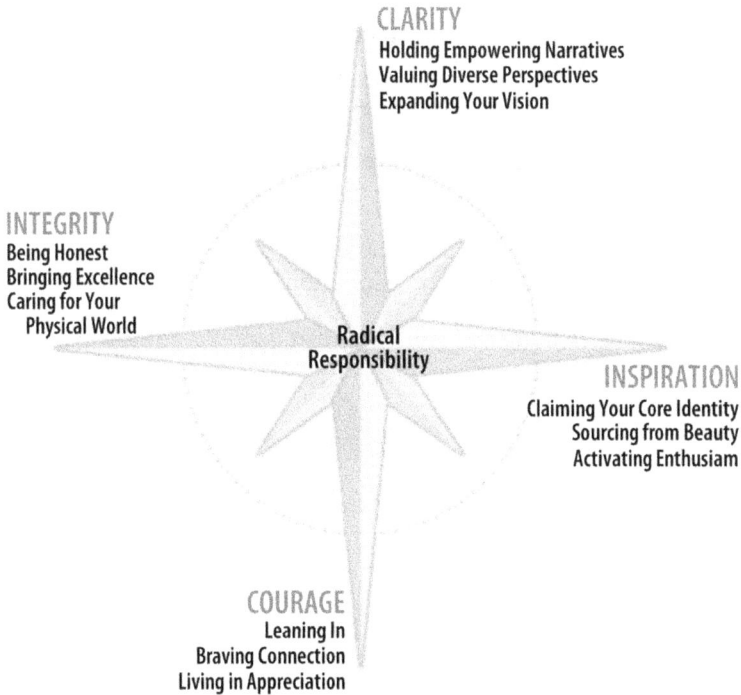

CLARITY
Holding Empowering Narratives
Valuing Diverse Perspectives
Expanding Your Vision

INTEGRITY
Being Honest
Bringing Excellence
Caring for Your
    Physical World

Radical
Responsibility

INSPIRATION
Claiming Your Core Identity
Sourcing from Beauty
Activating Enthusiam

COURAGE
Leaning In
Braving Connection
Living in Appreciation

Warm-up Questions

- How passionate—*how on fire*—am I in my life?

- How clearly can I articulate the core values and sense of purpose that guide me?

- To what degree do I consciously pay attention to the beauty around me as a source of inspiration in my life?

- Do I tend more toward being arrogant, or toward playing myself down?

~ Chapter Three ~

Inspiration

INSPIRATION IS THE DISCIPLINE OF cultivating your spiritual life as a source of aliveness and creativity. It is imbedded in and infused by the sense that we are spiritual beings—that spirituality is an essential part of who we are, and that it both deeply enriches our experience of life and enhances our leadership presence.

What Inspiration is: attuning to your spirit
What Inspiration does: activates meaning and aliveness
Distortion: arrogance
Repression: self-deflation

Metaphorically understood in many wisdom traditions, Inspiration is being connected to a brightness or light inside you, and letting that light be seen and felt by others. It is being aware of and turned on by the spiritual source of your life, whatever you understand that source to be. It is depending on that Life-Source to guide and sustain you from the inside out.

On the Medicine Wheel, Inspiration sits in the East, the place of the rising sun. Many ancient cultures held the sun as sacred, a representation of divinity. Their spiritual lives were very closely connected to their physical experience, and they experienced the sun as the most powerful force in their physical/spiritual lives. From the perspective of physics and biology, this is literally true and always has been. The light from the sun is the energy source for all life on the planet. It makes sense that almost all modern spiritual and religious traditions associate the Light with the divine.

Inspiration Archetypes: Sovereign and Mystic

The Sovereign (Queen/King) in you is the one who claims authority in your own life, is deeply connected to a clear set of core values and a compelling sense of purpose. This is the part of you that is confident, but not arrogant, authoritative without being dictatorial. The one who, while acknowledging the power of who you are, is in service to the larger community and something greater than egoic self.

The Mystic in you is the one who acknowledges the power of invisible creative forces, whether recognized as God, the laws of quantum physics, or something else, whether identified as spiritual or energetic. This is the part of you that knows there are unseen Universal forces operating behind everything, and feels connected to those forces. It is the part of you that is inspired and compelled by beauty, and lives in a state of enthusiasm generated by inner forces of gratitude and optimism.

Recall that archetypes are universally recognized energetic signatures. They represent a whole constellation of attitudes, skills, and ways of being with a particular genius to them.

Take a moment now to visualize and feel the Sovereign and Mystic in you—and the degrees to which you are familiar with them and have access to their particular energies.

The Core Practices of Inspiration

Claiming Your Core Identity

Claiming your core Identity is identifying and keeping yourself connected to what most deeply defines you. To the larger context for your life—from values to purpose to how you perceive your place in the Universe.

Sourcing from Beauty

Sourcing from beauty is tuning into the beauty all around you, including in yourself and others—as well as cultivating and evoking that beauty—as a source of ongoing inspiration for your life.

Activating Enthusiasm

Activating a deep sense of aliveness in yourself—through practices like gratitude, celebration and authentic desire.

Practice Elements

Claiming Your Core Identity

- » Knowing your place in the Universe
- » Identifying your core values
- » Articulating your life purpose

Sourcing from Beauty

- » Cultivating a sense of awe
- » Attuning to beauty
- » Evoking beauty

Activating Enthusiasm

» Practicing gratitude

» Celebrating life

» Listening to your desire

Reactive Patterns of Inspiration

Arrogance

Self-Deflation

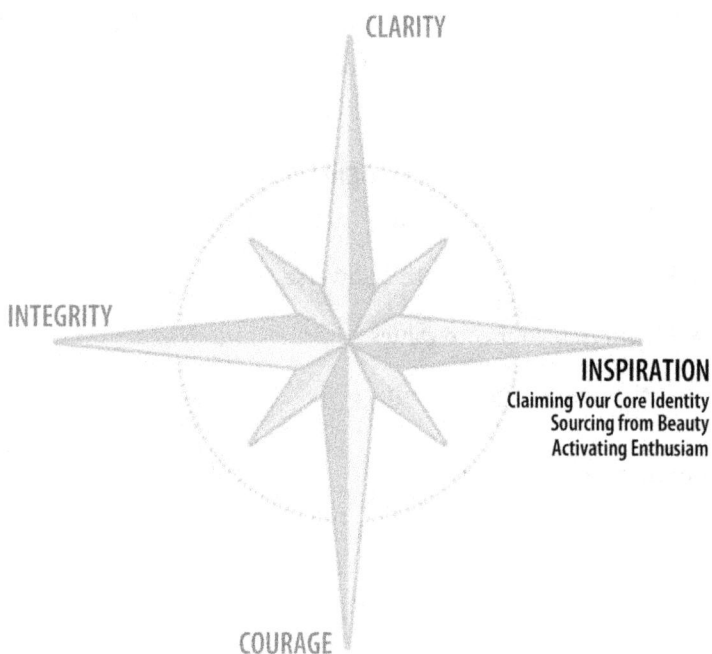

CLARITY

INTEGRITY

INSPIRATION
Claiming Your Core Identity
Sourcing from Beauty
Activating Enthusiam

COURAGE

Claiming Your Core Identity

There is a kind of inheritance—a core identity—that is the spirit you came into the world with. To practice the discipline of Inspiration—to show up as an inspired human being—requires that you come to know and claim this spiritual inheritance.

Claiming your core identity is the practice of defining and connecting with, in an ongoing way, primarily three things: your cosmology or sense of belonging in the universe, your core values, and your unique purpose in life.

To claim your identity on a spiritual level requires a kind of knowing that is imaginal. Your cosmology, core values, and purpose must be personally, subjectively, and uniquely imagined.

Years ago, a client and I were sitting by a mountain lake together, preparing for his upcoming 3-day wilderness vision quest. A big raven flew overhead and let out a guttural sound, as only ravens can do. After a few moments, my client says, "I've never shared this with anyone because it sounds a little crazy, but I feel a special connection to ravens. And when that raven flew over, I had the feeling it was sending me a message. But then I wonder, is this just my imagination? Am I making this up? Maybe it's random and means nothing. So which is it—imagined or real?"

My response was something like this: "Well, since neither one of those options—imagined or real—is objectively true, you get to choose the one that gives you the richer experience."

The Universe is full of magic if you choose to see it that way. Was the message from the raven a figment of my client's imagination, or was it real? Yes, and yes. Imagination gives us access to the realms of the intangible. It is what we rely on to know the "truth" of a religion, a theology, or a spiritual path—which, while not empirically provable, are nevertheless real, and can be sources of immense power and inspiration.

When we turn imagination toward ourselves and questions of

who we really are, it gives us access to the deeper highly subjective dimensions of ourselves, which if we are to create a meaningful reality, are essential realms for us to access.

When you go to this place inside yourself—perhaps thought of as the esoteric, or the abstract, or the place of soul—in search of your cosmology, your values, and your purpose, you find a powerful spiritual foundation for creating a life that is truly yours, and genuinely expresses who you are. Your imagination supports you in being the author of your own life, which begins with interpreting your identity and your experience in ways that enrich and empower you. You get to choose how to define who you are in a way that gives you the richer experience.

Knowing Your Place In the Universe

What you believe about the nature of the universe—including life on this planet—and your place in the scheme of things, is your cosmology. Your cosmology tells a story about how the universe came to be, where human beings come from, and why we're here. In essence, your cosmology is a system of belief that helps you make sense of life.

If you're a religious person, your cosmology is largely articulated for you in the beliefs/principles/practices of your religion. Whether that's the case or not, It is still important for you to consciously choose what you believe about the nature of the Universe and your place in it, and articulate that for yourself in your own words, in a way that feels good, true, and compelling to you.

Ultimately, the importance of your cosmology is the way it shapes your identity and how you live. Are you atheist, agnostic, Christian, Muslim, pagan? What you choose, including choosing not to choose, makes a difference in how you live.

Einstein is reported to have said the most important question we each can ask ourselves is whether we think the universe is a friendly place or not. While there does not appear to be first-hand evidence that he actually said this, it remains as an example of the impact of cosmology on how we live. How you choose to live, and how you respond to what happens in life, reflects your system of beliefs about the universe—that it's cruel, Godless, random, full of meaning, supportive of human evolution and goodness, friendly, or something else. I often have clients tell me they believe that things happen for a reason. I don't know if this is true. I just know that their belief that it's true has an impact on how they choose to think, feel, and live.

PARADIGM SHIFT ALERT
From: What you believe about the Universe and your place in it is an esoteric discussion with no practical relevance to the way you live or lead.
To: Your identity, the choices you make, and how you live your life, are significantly shaped by what you believe about the Universe and your place in it.

Identifying Your Core Values

Early in any executive coaching engagement, my clients identify and claim their 3-5 core values. This is absolutely fundamental and foundational to the rest of their leadership journey, and the rest of their life for that matter.

For most of my clients, it isn't the first time they've been asked to clarify their values. It is, however, usually the first time they've been asked to dig below the surface of their intellect and draw their values out of their deepest intuitive sense of who they are and what they're up to in this life.

This kind of values exploration is not an exercise. It's a conversation with one's core self. To frame the conversation, I ask clients to look through two lenses. 1) The values you choose must be relevant guiding principles in all areas of your life, not just in your work. 2) The words you choose to express your values must do two somewhat paradoxical things at once—describe who you absolutely and essentially already are, while at the same time challenge you to be all that you aspire to be.

Your core values are how you define yourself. Instead of looking to the world out there—the expectations and opinions of others—to define you, your core values conversation causes you to look inside yourself for who you are and what matters most.

The more deeply introspective you are when you identify your core values, and the more they energize you when you reflect on them, the more practically useful they are to you in everyday life.

The degree to which your values inspire and energize you is often the degree to which they have been tested. Do you choose your value of honesty over the easy way out? Do you choose your value of love when you are tempted to hate?

Your values are also tested when they compete inside your own value system. If you value both compassion and justice, how do you honor them both?

The more you reflect on your values, and ask yourself how you can best honor them in real-life situations, the more they drive the ways you think, feel, and act.

Articulating Your Life Purpose

Knowing and articulating your purpose in life can be a powerful inspiration, as well as litmus test, for the choices you make—from friendships to profession to the ways you spend your time and energy.

To discover your purpose, ask who you are on the planet to *be*, rather than the particular job you're here to do, or career to pursue. That said, since your doing ideally flows from your *being*, your awareness of purpose inspires your career trajectory as well as your day-to-day living and relating.

Theologian Frederick Buechner, in *Wishful Thinking: A Theological ABC*, says "the place God calls you to is the place where your deep gladness and the world's deep hunger meet."

In other words, your purpose is a confluence of what you're *built for*, and what you *stand for*. What you're built for is your unique combination of passion and talents, or what Buechner calls your gladness. What you stand for is the kind of world you want to help create—the world's hunger, as you perceive it.

Your purpose is something you discover. It is not something you *make up*. It is, rather, your *makeup*, an aspect of your core identity. Articulating your purpose challenges you to crystallize your understanding of the nature of your particular spiritual makeup.

To live your purpose is to offer it as a gift to others—which requires that you fully embrace it as yours to give.

And yet, I have experienced both in myself and in my clients as we dive deep into the purpose conversation, that it's not so easy to fully embrace the purpose that is essential to our nature. There is a resistance that we can often trace back to childhood. When you were a kid, and people wanted to bring you down a notch, they said, "Who do you think you are, God's gift to the world?" That's a hard put-down to let go of. But the truth is, you *are* God's gift to the world. The fact that each of us came into in this world is evidence enough. The question is whether we will remember the gifts we carry—and keep choosing to offer them—in each moment.

So what does it mean to fully embrace the spiritual power of your purpose? It means to keep it in front of you. Reflect on it daily. Make it part of your self-image. Ask if and how you are honoring it. Your purpose is the particular way that you belong to the community of life. How are you honoring, or not honoring, that sense of belonging?

ACTIVATION QUESTIONS
- What would it look like to honor one of my core values in this moment?
- What kind of image of myself am I holding? What impact is it having on me and others?

Sourcing from Beauty

"I want to know if you can see beauty even when it is not pretty every day, and if you can source your life from its presence."
Oriah Mountain Dreamer, The Invitation

Beauty is the way human beings most directly experience divine presence. While this may seem like a radical statement, it explains why sourcing from beauty is one of the core practices of Inspiration. While we experience beauty in our physical environment, including the people around us, and beauty seems to be possessed by tangible things, it is absolutely intangible. Beauty is one way of experiencing and talking about the form that spirit takes.

In case it's not yet obvious, let's be clear that we're defining beauty in a much broader and deeper way than the fashion-magazine-beauty of popular culture. Let's also make the connection right away between beauty and leadership. The human spirit is oriented to beauty. Therefore, if you want to engage people in any enterprise on the level of the human spirit, your work needs to be infused with beauty. Beauty creates a feeling of wellbeing. It makes us more resistant to boredom and depletion, and supports our aliveness and resilience.

PARADIGM SHIFT ALERT
From: Beauty is cosmetic, and tangential to the important things in life and leadership.
To: Beauty is spiritual substance in physical form. It inspires creative energy. It ignites and lifts the human spirit, which is critical to the success of any life, and any enterprise.

When you source your life from the presence of beauty—when you're more intentional about connecting with beauty wherever you are—you're in turn inspired to make the world, including your home or office, a more beautiful place.

One aspect of embracing leadership as a sacred trust is to encourage greater expression and fuller experience of beauty on the planet. What practical difference would that attitude and practice make in your relationships, the way you communicate, the way you design products and human systems, and the way you solve problems?

Cultivating a Sense of Awe

Beauty has always been one of the most direct and powerful ways that human beings sense the presence of a larger-than-us creative force in the Universe. The wisdom traditions and religious texts are full of references to God being seen and known through natural beauty.

I'll never forget one evening in the mountains of Virginia. I'm sitting with a friend on a rock outcropping watching a particularly gorgeous sunset. We're silent, transfixed, soaking in the colors. And suddenly, she's clapping and yelling out, "Yay, God!"

Have you ever had the impulse, in the presence of awe-inspiring Nature, to applaud the Creator? There are times when our awe of natural beauty connects us directly to its Source. You know this if you have ever looked at the stars or the ocean, and felt infinitesimally small, and at the same time part of something incredibly vast and great. That sense of being an infinitesimal part of an infinite Universe can inspire a sense of your own spirit being an expression of a larger Spirit.

There are human-made parallels to awe-inspiring natural beauty. The Golden Gate Bridge, the Eiffel Tower, the Sydney Opera House, and great works of art. There are also human expressions of beauty. A ballet move, a perfect dive off the 10 meter platform, a leap and catch in the end-zone, or the discovery of Velcro. How are we humans capable of such beauty? When we witness it, our spirits soar. We're inspired!

> *"Those who dwell...among the beauties and mysteries of the earth are never alone or weary of life."*
>
> Rachel Carson, *A Sense of Wonder*

To "dwell among the beauties and mysteries of the earth" is not a matter of location, it's a matter of attention. Wherever you are, look for what is awe-inspiring to you. It could be a snow-capped mountain peak, a perfectly struck corner kick, the silence in a grove of giant redwood trees, or the sip of wine you just took.

PARADIGM SHIFT ALERT
From: Awe is something that happens to you in response to something powerful in your world or experience.
To: While awe is often something that happens to you, it is even more powerful as a choice you make— a choice to bring a powerful quality of attention to your world and your experience.

Grand expressions of beauty are relatively easy to recognize and be in awe of. The mountain peak for example. The more *quiet beauty* that lives in your sip of wine takes more attention. It's the artwork hanging in the coffee house that you could easily miss. The color of new leaves in the spring. The lines on the face of someone you love. All these things can be awe-inspiring—if you choose to be awe-inspired. And when you do, your aliveness meter goes up. A little more light comes into your being.

Attuning to Beauty

Beauty truly is in the eye of the beholder—existing in your perception. While beauty begins with sensory input, it is completely dependent on the interpretations you give to that sensation. Consider the taste of food for example. Your taste buds interact with the food, but in most cases, with the exception of spoiled foods, the qualities of delicious or bland or yucky are in your mouth and mind, not in the food itself. This is very personal to you, and at the same time reflects the culture and micro-cultures you are part of. So beauty exists as your perception, influenced by your personality, and at the same time your culture.

Perceiving beauty comes naturally to us. But it can be heightened and refined with intentionality—by attuning to it. Which means sensitizing ourselves to the resonance or dissonance we experience inside ourselves in response to our environment, to other people, and our own thoughts and feelings.

Why is this relevant? How does understanding beauty and attuning to it relate to being an inspiring leader, and living an inspired life? Why pay attention to what you find beautiful and what you find ugly? It's primarily two things—self-awareness and spiritual aliveness.

The self-awareness informed by beauty can take many forms. What you find beautiful can tell you something about your personality, sensibilities, and values. For example, you might realize that you find old buildings more beautiful than modern ones, signaling a value perhaps for history and tradition. Or abstract art, which might reveal a personality oriented to out-of-the-box thinking or quirkiness. What you discover about yourself can guide choices you make about the environment you live and work in, the people you spend time with, the work and tasks you are involved with, and how you spend your leisure time. This isn't about judging these things as good or bad, but about making choices from a more complete and nuanced sense of self.

Attuning to beauty includes paying attention to what you find ugly. Observe when you experience dissonance, even if only mildly. This is valuable information. It helps you see what you don't want to give your life energy to, and what you don't want to perpetuate in your life, family, or organization.

In addition to self-awareness, attuning to beauty enlivens you. When you perceive beauty, your neurological system gets a little jolt of energy, creating a feeling of greater aliveness. It's almost like beauty plucks the guitar strings of your energetic being, waking up your spirit. Your awakened spirit shines brighter and makes you feel better about yourself and more compelling for others to be around. You experience greater richness, resilience, and inspiration.

Years ago, I conducted a four-day leadership development program for a leader and his team in Venezuela. On the third evening, at our all-team celebration dinner, this gentleman introduced me, as the visitor from the States, to a Venezuelan rum that he took great pleasure as well as great pride in. I had come to know him as an inspiring person, and effective leader. I won't say that his taste in fine rum, or his nuanced technique of using his breath to get the maximum pleasure from it, was the secret to his success and influence. But I dare say that his attention to beauty and the richness it brings to his life is part of what makes him an enlivening leader to be around.

Evoking Beauty

A big benefit of awakening your sense of awe and paying attention to what you resonate with and what you don't, is that these two practices tend to evoke beauty in the world around you.

To more intentionally evoke beauty is to do three things. One is to recognize it in ourselves, and bring that to the surface. Another is bringing it out in others. And a third is inspiring behaviors that make our world a more beautiful place.

Let's start with your own beauty. The practice of attuning to beauty is a practice of recognition. It is recognizing qualities in the beauty around you that you are willing to claim in yourself—qualities that enhance your life and impact. I vividly recall a moment, as a young man and counselor at a summer camp, sitting in the dawn silence on the lakeshore. As I looked out at the mist rising off the glassy water, I saw in that stillness there a kind of calm that I began to see was available to me, and perhaps already existed in me, waiting to be more fully revealed and claimed. The beauty of the lake was awakening an aspect of the nobility of my own spirit.

I'm certainly not alone in this kind of experience. I have heard it from many people, including my own vision-quest clients, who have similarly encountered an aspect of their nobility in the beauty of nature, whether it's evoked by a snow-capped peak, a humming-bird visit, or an elk walking through their campsite. Not only have they become more connected to their own nobility, but they have had a-ha moments and creative ideas stimulated by their experience of beauty.

A second aspect of evoking beauty is seeing it in others, and bringing it out in them. With every human being, and in every moment, we have a choice—to see their beauty or to see their ugliness. The beautiful and the ugly, the noble and the profane, live side by side in every human being. Both are visible. The question is what we choose to perceive, and what we choose to focus on.

When we focus on the beauty in people, we bring it out in them. Our choice of what to perceive in another becomes a mirror, which gives them a reflection of their best self, invites them to identify with that self, and to live from it. When you see beauty in others, your seeing boosts their self-esteem, their confidence, and their willingness to let their light shine. Your practice of seeing beauty in another makes their nobility of spirit more visible in the world.

That gift of reflecting another's beauty to them expands the notion that beauty is in the eye of the beholder. It makes beauty also in the *being* of the beholder—meaning that the beauty you see is connected to the beauty that you are. You can't see beauty outside yourself without a certain sensitivity inside yourself to that beauty. That sensitivity is part of your particular substance as a human being. That substance is part of who you are as a leader. It is part of your self-confidence, part of what inspires others about you, and part of what enables you to inspire the best in others.

It is also something that enables you to build strong relationships. Your practice of seeing beauty in others not only brings it out in them, it makes you more open to connecting with them, and them with you—not only in terms of emotional bonding, but also receptivity to one another's ideas and ability to manage conflict with grace.

PARADIGM SHIFT ALERT
From: Acknowledging your own inner or outer beauty is vanity.
To: Being aware of and acknowledging your own inner and outer beauty is essential to the kind of confidence that attracts others to you, inspires them, and enables you to see and mirror to them their own beauty.

Leadership as a sacred trust hinges in large part on our ability to evoke the beauty of spirit and character in every person we interact with. One of my executive client's life purpose statement is, "I am a force for human dignity and light, seen and revered." This is what he orients himself toward every day. It's at the heart of who he is as a leader.

A third key aspect of evoking beauty is the way it inspires action. As we evoke the beauty that lives in ourselves and others, it is more available to come out in our thoughts, feelings, words, and actions. Another way of saying this is that when you attune to beauty, you reward what you find beautiful with behaviors that honor it. For example, a greater attunement to beauty may cause you to hang not just any art on the wall, but art that brings a certain specific quality or aesthetic that you want to experience in the space. Or you clean up the mess in the kitchen because your sensitivity to what's beautiful, and what's not, demands action. Or you get involved in protecting a wilderness area, or river, or ocean. Or you make changes in your office environment that enliven people's spirit and creativity, rather than deaden it.

Charles Eisenstein, philosopher and author of *Sacred Economics*, writes about the yearning in human beings to create "the more beautiful world our hearts know is possible." What resonates with me about this idea is the notion that our sense of beauty is also a call to action. And the opportunities to take action to preserve beauty in the world, or to make the world a more beautiful place, are as expansive as our sensibilities and imagination.

ACTIVATION QUESTIONS
- How attuned to beauty am I right now?
- What can I do in this moment to evoke beauty in myself and in the people and world around me?

Activating Enthusiasm

The word enthusiasm literally means *"in theos,"* or "in God/ Life." Enthusiasm then, is moment by moment, choosing to be in love with the world, and with Life, in the largest sense of the word. It is choosing joy as the dominant spiritual thread of the tapestry that is your life.

There's a kind of enthusiasm that gets activated when a person, idea, thing, experience, or event grabs you. There's also a kind of enthusiasm that you *activate in yourself.* Rather than waiting for enthusiasm to happen to you, you intentionally cultivate qualities that fire you up, like gratitude, celebration, and attention to desire. When you do that, enthusiasm is more a *practice in your life* than a *response to your life.*

PARADIGM SHIFT ALERT

From: Enthusiasm is a feeling caused by something exciting happening. In other words, it is *caused by your life.*

To: Enthusiasm is something you cultivate in yourself. In other words, it is a *practice in your life.*

Practicing Gratitude

In the summer of 1998, I spent 20 days alone in the northern Minnesota wilderness. I was on a spiritual quest. In the years leading up to it, I had discovered that I no longer fully resonated with the spiritual tradition I had grown up with—so I was looking for new spiritual ground to stand on. After 20 days of reading, journaling, and deep contemplation in the wilderness, to my surprise I found that for me it all came down to one word—gratitude. I had discovered that gratitude kept showing up as an essential practice in all the spiritual traditions, and was invariably acknowledged as the essence of powerful prayer. The more I reflected on it, the more I saw that gratitude could be the central tenet of my spirituality. Because in its essence, gratitude is acknowledging the presence of the divine in the world, in you, and in your life.

There is a depth to gratitude that is connected to the privilege of being alive. Giving thanks for your life builds your life force, and strengthens your relationship with Life itself. It's hard to be deflated or down when you're feeling grateful for your life, and all that it contains.

Start with small things. Don't wait for something monumental. In fact, don't wait at all. Give thanks for what's right in front of you. Your coffee in the morning, the smile lines around your spouse's eyes, the fact that your car works.

Experiment also with being grateful for something *before* it shows up in your experience. Be truly grateful for the bond of love you have with your teenager, especially when that relationship feels strained, and see what impact it has on your interactions. Be truly grateful for the people you work with—then pay attention to the subtle changes in how you relate to them.

Out of the soil of gratitude springs optimism. You can be optimistic *because* you've heard good news. But it's even more powerful to be optimistic *before* you've heard good news—to send brain waves of gratitude out into the world before you see the outcomes that warrant them. The optimism flowing from gratitude attracts opportunity because when you are optimistic, you focus more on possibilities than on problems. You put your attention on the possibility of good things, experiences, and people coming toward to you, which makes it all more likely.

Gratitude, and the optimism it fosters, is an attitude of expectation and assuredness that Life holds good things for you—that

Life "has your back." This is not easy when you're facing major road-blocks, setbacks, or breakdowns. And yet, it's in those times that practicing gratitude is particularly powerful. Focusing on the blessings in your life, and your thankfulness for them, makes you more receptive to creative ideas and solutions to problems.

If you want to attract good things into your life, give thanks for them before they arrive. The times when the difficult circumstances of your life argue against gratitude are the times when you most need it—as a powerful force that goes beyond acknowledging the blessings in life to creating them. To activate gratitude as a creator of good things, experiment with giving thanks, as crazy as that might seem, for the challenges and disappointments of Life. Give thanks for the things that really annoy you, as if they are here to help you learn more about yourself, help you grow, and challenge you to practice compassion. Give thanks for the pain and loss in life. Not from a "no pain, no gain" perspective, or with a "grin and bear it" attitude, but from a willingness to embrace loss as a catalyst for your spiritual growth.

PARADIGM SHIFT ALERT
From: Gratitude is reserved for acknowledging good things that have occurred.
To: Gratitude acknowledges good things. But more significantly, it is a force that attracts good things to you.

Celebrating Life

Early in my coaching career I participated in a year-long series of retreats to develop my leadership presence. At one pivotal moment our workshop leader looked me fiercely and playfully in the eyes and said, "Burke, it's time to stop working it, and start digging it."

In that moment, all the ways I had been trying so hard throughout my life to be better, or be something I thought I wasn't, flashed through my mind. And I faced the possibility of letting that all go for a different way—a way of deeply enjoying life instead of working so hard at it—a way of celebration.

I began to see digging it, or celebrating life, as being connected to what turns me on. You know you're turned on when your eyes light up. You know it when you feel excited and energized.

I've come to see this way of celebration as having three levels. Level one is responding to an obvious reason to celebrate—when something triggers a joyful feeling in you, and there's cause for celebration. Level one includes acknowledging wins—ideally both big and small; and other meaningful moments of your life, like holidays, birthdays, graduations—all the things you buy Hallmark™ cards for. The opportunity with level one celebration is to do it more often, and more consciously—meaning in ways that make you feel more vibrant and connected to the pleasure of being alive—rather than in ways that feel more like numbing out or escaping from life.

Level two celebration is of life itself, for no other reason than the fact that you're alive. My wife and I have a favorite restaurant in Crested Butte, Colorado—the Sunflower. Its owner is the epitome of someone who celebrates life. When we walk in she greets us with big hugs and a warmth and enthusiasm that completely fills us up with a sense of life is good. We marvel at the way she goes about her work, making it look and feel more like a party than a job. She's an example of celebrating life no matter where you are or what you're doing—of living each day, and even each moment, as something to celebrate, versus something to take for granted or something to endure.

I have found many opportunities for level-two celebration. My swim workouts, for example. Something changes when I approach the workout as a celebration. The family dinner is an opportunity. So are your Monday-morning team meetings. Making love. Driving your child to school. With some awareness and intentionality, the possibilities for celebrating life are endless.

A third level of celebration asks a lot of us, and is highly empowering in return. It's celebrating when you really don't feel like it—when the circumstances of your life are anything but causes for celebration—when life is evoking anger, pain, and grief. Consider the possibility that, even in these moments, there is still a type of celebration that appreciates the fact that you can feel life intensely. I'm not talking about whitewashing. I'm talking about adding a dimension to your life that has the potential to transform it.

Some people are uncomfortable with celebration—often because they equate it with being too proud, too boisterous, or too showy. Or they simply think it's a waste of time. The truth is, however, that celebration is good for the spirit. It creates a positive energy—whether it's just inside you, or in your family, or on your business team—that makes wins, opportunities, and the good things in life more likely to come your way.

If you're one of the resisters, just know two things. One, that celebration does not have to be loud, or even visible. You can celebrate quietly and authentically with a smile, a quiet acknowledgment, or an affirming handshake. And two, it's worth it. Joy and celebration make life more full, meaningful, and fun.

Listening to Your Desire

A third element of activating enthusiasm is letting your desire have a voice. Many spiritual traditions teach us to be suspicious of what we want, and to see our desires as antithetical to a genuine spirituality. But consider the possibility that what you most authentically want may reveal ways that your spirit is trying to get nourished, and ways that your spirit is attempting to be expressed in the world.

Consider the possibility that your spirit-based desires (vs. your more persona-driven preferences) are an important part of your relationship with Life; and that listening to those desires, whether you act on them or not, is a way of being faithful to your destiny— not destiny meaning fate, but destiny meaning the unfolding of your life in a way that authentically expresses who you are.

PARADIGM SHIFT ALERT
From: Desires are selfish and egoic—to be kept *in check*.
To: Desires may be indicators of our essential identity trying to express itself in the world. They are to be *checked-in* with.

One of the ways we talk about someone who is enthusiastic, or passionate about fully expressing themselves and their creative drive, is to say they're hungry. In other words, they're full of desire. Not mild desire, but intense desire. To be hungry is an essential part of an enthusiastic, spiritually turned-on life.

And yet our hunger, our desire, is often muted. As human beings, we are essentially domesticated animals. By the time we are adults, much of our authentic desire has been trained out of us. And yet, there's both power and inspiration available in your desire, waiting to be unmuzzled. We can learn from wild animals, incapable of being anything other than their authentic selves, doing what they're designed to do, living in response to their nature, and the desires that flow from that nature. They know exactly what they want, and have no idea what it is to censor their desire.

Most of us humans, on the other hand, in our generally-tame lives, listen more to what we *should* want than to what we *actually* want. The more this is true of you, the less life force you have access to.

One of the reasons that we default to a *should-want* orientation, and a tendency to live more by convention than by desire, is that we don't distinguish between wild hunger, and wild behavior. While wild behavior can get a bad rap, wild desire in its pure form is sacred. Decoupled from acting it out, authentic desire is always something to be honored for the life force it contains.

Alongside your deepest desires, pay attention to what you really *don't* want. What you find wildly disgusting—versus merely annoying—can just as powerfully connect you to your enthusiasm as your desire can. Instead of forcing yourself to live by the rule of think something nice, or don't think anything at all, let yourself have moments of disgust. What do you really not want, and why? When you dig a little into what turns you off, you may find some powerful insights into who you are, what turns you on, and what inspires you.

Your deep desire is like the wild man or wild woman inside you, urging you to live life large. Pay attention to him or her. When you sense your enthusiasm for life waning, ask yourself what you really want. Seek out an activity you've always wanted to do, act on a desire you would normally suppress, or express something you really want to say that you would normally keep to yourself.

ACTIVATION QUESTIONS
- How am I celebrating life today?
- What do I think I *should* want? What do I *truly* want?

Arrogance and Self-Deflation

(The Reactive Patterns of Inspiration)

Inspiration is being intimately connected to your spirit and all that it offers to you and your world. Its reactive patterns of *arrogance* and *self-deflation* are both easy traps to fall prey to. They are pervasive, and yet not always obvious. Consider both arrogance and self-deflation as two forms of *separation from your spirit*—of getting distracted by your smaller insecure self, and thus losing connection to your spiritual Self, your highest values, and larger reason for being.

Remember, as you read about arrogance and self-deflation, that we all are subject to reactivity from time to time through lack of awareness and intention. The inner adventure is to catch ourselves in reaction, and in the spirit of radical responsibility, choose the Discipline over the distortion or repression.

Arrogance (Inspiration Distorted)

Arrogance can look like Inspiration, but is actually a façade of it—a distortion.

Holding yourself superior—I didn't think I had a drop of arrogance in me until my wife gently pointed it out. It was after a small dinner party. We were washing the dishes, and she asked why I had been so quiet during the evening. I said I hadn't had much to say, and she pushed back with the thought that maybe I wasn't interested in the conversation, and that my far-away energy gave the impression that I felt the tone of conversation was "beneath" me and not worth contributing to. It wasn't easy to acknowledge, but I couldn't really deny the truth in it.

Since then, I've been more aware of the ways that I hold myself *above* or superior to the conversation, and thus withhold myself from it. Now that I can see the dynamic, I look for ways to bring my perspective in as a contribution, rather than sit on the sidelines.

Superiority makes your self-esteem dependent on others being less than you. Your subconscious mind thinks being superior lifts you up in others' eyes, or makes you important, but instead it makes you a bore to be around. Superiority can lead you to offer unwelcome advice. You may be trying to help, but you're actually getting in the way of another's growth. Superiority keeps you from learning from others because in your mind they have nothing to offer that you don't already know.

Creating separation—When you're arrogant, you deny the brilliance and beauty of life around you. You think it's all about you. In those moments of arrogance, however rare or common they are, you're unaware of or disconnected from your relationship with the larger sphere of Life. You make yourself all important and the larger-than-you Universe almost irrelevant.

When you're inspired, your connection to Life is one of the things that draws people to you, and creates connection. When arrogance shows up, the opposite occurs. It creates separation—and resistance—in the people around you. No one likes to collaborate with a braggart, or someone who hogs the limelight or claims all the credit.

Arrogance also creates a state of disconnection from yourself, which can sap your energy. Instead of feeling centered in yourself, and connected to your own life force and essential nature, you waste life energy on posturing and maintaining a pretense of being something or someone you're not.

Taking yourself too seriously—A component of arrogance is taking yourself too seriously. You get myopic in your frame of reference. You look through a filter of getting your persona validated.

Instead, look through the eyes of your spirit, which is primarily interested in participating as fully as possible in the larger movement of Life. Taking yourself less seriously doesn't mean you get smaller. It means you get larger. You get large enough to stop making it about you—how important you are, how over worked you are, how unfairly treated you are, how surrounded by idiots you are.

When you take yourself less seriously, you can actually take life more seriously—which doesn't mean approaching life with a heaviness or sense of burden, but with a sense of intensely committed delight in the gifts and opportunities that life is offering you in any moment.

Taking yourself too seriously is related to taking things personally, which impedes your spiritual growth. There's an arrogance to taking things personally because, whether you mean to or not, you are seeing everything as a reflection of you. When you realize that not everything has to do with you, you can participate in life from a much freer place, where you're less concerned about validating your persona vis-à-vis the world around you, and more interested in listening to the guidance of your own spirit to create your experience in the world.

Fake confidence—Ironically, arrogance is actually a lack of confidence. It comes from an underlying insecurity that you don't have another way of compensating for. Because the feeling of not being enough is mostly unconscious, it is difficult to see in yourself. But when you do see it, rather than trying to stop being arrogant, get curious about what insecurity you might be covering up. Then look for ways to transform the part of you that lacks confidence.

The difference between arrogance and confidence is that true confidence is you validating you. Your self-validation comes from being connected to your essential nature, to your strengths, and even to your vulnerabilities. In arrogance, you look to external measures for validation—in the form of achievement and success as defined by the world around you.

By the world's standards is the key phrase here. When you achieve and succeed by your own standards, it builds true confidence. It can be natural and healthy to tie your confidence to your achievement. But when too closely connected, you can become de-spirited when faced with failings of any degree.

Confidence tied to achievement can give you a kind of swagger, which can be healthy or distorted. The question to hold is, "Does your swagger diminish others or inspire them?"

PARADIGM SHIFT ALERT
From: Arrogance is supreme confidence.
To: Arrogance is masked insecurity.

The irony of playing small—Arrogance may look like you're playing big, but it's actually the opposite. Instead of generosity of spirit, arrogance is smallness of spirit. Out of insecurity, arrogance has you claim to own the place, and be better than others. An inflated persona just looks big because it's all puffed up, but with little substance.

When you play small through arrogance, you constrict the flow of inspiration in your life. It's like tying a knot in a water hose. The wisdom that you could be experiencing—whether from others or your own internal depths—is constricted by being more interested in appearances than growth. Feeling insecure in yourself and protecting your image can cause you to dismiss what others have to offer you. It can also limit what you deem them worthy of receiving from you.

Self-Deflation (Inspiration Repressed)

You can also play small through self-deflation. Like arrogance, self-deflation is self-limiting and diminishes your experience and impact in life. Self-deflation might seem to honor Spirit, and keep you from blowing your persona out of proportion, but it actually limits the strength of your connection to Spirit, and thus detracts from how inspired your life is.

When you self-deflate, you reject your gifts, dishonoring their Source. You hold yourself apart from, and resist identifying with, the grandeur of the Universe that underpins your life.

When we're arrogant, we hold ourselves superior to the brilliance and beauty of life around us. When we self-deflate, we deny that greatness inside us. Either way, we hold ourselves separate, and make it all about us.

PARADIGM SHIFT ALERT

From: Self-deflation is a good thing because it keeps you humble and makes others feel comfortable around you.

To: Self-deflation is damaging to you because it limits your ability to create the life and impact you want to have, and damaging to others because it diminishes the opportunity for them to be inspired by who you are.

Like arrogance, self-deflation comes from a sense of smallness and insecurity, and a lack of self-esteem and confidence. While the unconscious voice of arrogance sounds like, "I own the place, and I'm better than you," self-deflation whispers "I don't have a place, and I have little to offer."

When you dip into the reactive mindset of self-deflation, you lose touch with your energy for making a positive difference. Your energy goes to trying to prove yourself, rather than to making the contribution you're here to make. You're looking for external validation, and convinced that you won't get it because you'll never achieve enough by the world's standards.

You not only lose your own energy, but can become an energy suck to others. It's exhausting to try to build someone's self-esteem who thinks too little of themselves. When you become that person, you're not inspiring or enjoyable to be around. You miss out on connection and opportunities to collaborate—which further feeds a self-deflating vicious cycle.

Self-deflation often comes from, and/or contributes to, comparing yourself unfavorably to others. Rather than holding yourself superior, you assume inferiority, which tends to lead you straight into the trap of envy. To dip into envy is particularly toxic to your system. You want what others have—the skills, the money, the hunky husband or fashion-model wife, you name it. The type of desire that is envy comes from a mindset of lack versus a mindset of aspiration, wholeness, and claiming your nobility. Envy dampens your enthusiasm for life, whereas healthy desire is a source of enthusiasm. Envy sends your imagination spiraling down into deep black holes, imagining all the things you aren't, but you *should be*. It snuffs out confidence, takes you off your center, and shrinks the power of your presence.

There is a type of comparison that is healthy because it shines a light on what you aspire to. When you can compare from that place, rather than from a sense of self-deflation, you trigger learning and growth. You also cultivate connection with those you admire that is mutually beneficial because they feel your energy as affirming through appreciation rather than diminishing through envy.

PARADIGM SHIFT ALERT

From: Comparing yourself to others is a healthy type of self-awareness and way of measuring what you are achieving in life.

To: Comparing yourself to others sets up an unhealthy dynamic by either putting others on a pedestal and diminishing yourself, or feeling and acting superior to others.

ACTIVATION QUESTIONS

- In what ways is arrogance showing up and getting in my way?
- How am I diminishing myself? What would claiming my inherent nobility look like instead?

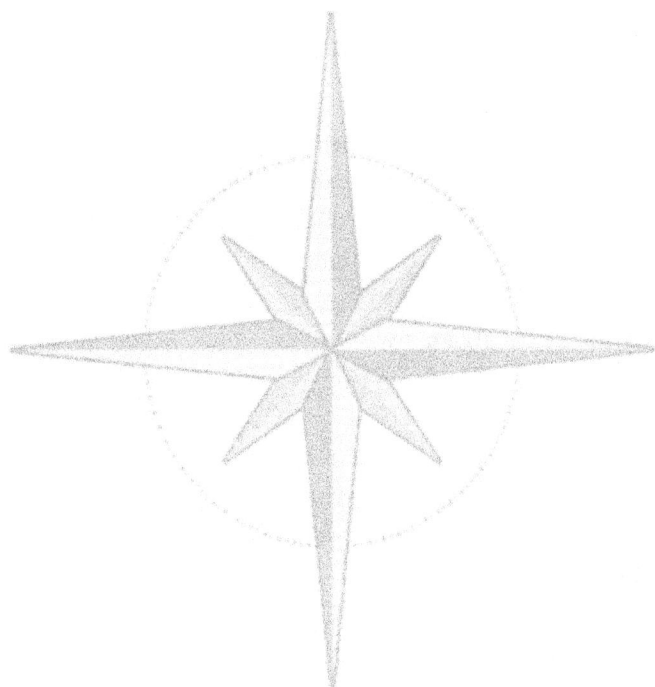

Chapter 3 Summary Points

The discipline of Inspiration is doing what it takes to be attuned to your spirit—to be on fire, and turned on.

Claiming Your Core Identity

Your core identity is what defines you at the deepest level—your core values, purpose, and sense of your place in the Universe. It is ultimately the basis of your self-authorship, and relies on your willingness to imagine. It is yours to make up, and yours to claim.

Sourcing from Beauty

Beauty creates an internal resonance that brings your spirit alive. With attention and intention, it can inspire you through your sense of awe, even with little things. Your life is enriched, and you enrich the lives of others, by both attuning to beauty and evoking it.

Activating Enthusiasm

Enthusiasm is "in-theos"—in God or Spirit. There are many flavors of enthusiasm. Whether it's optimism, gratitude, celebration, or authentic desire, enthusiasm can be a response to life. But even more powerfully, it is a stance in life—in other words, enthusiasm is something you intentionally activate in yourself in order to show up inspired.

Arrogance and Self-Deflation

Arrogance is the distortion of Inspiration. It takes the form of an inflated persona, trying to seem more confident than you are. Self-deflation is denying your true and natural nobility and being unwilling to claim your self-authority. Both arrogance and self-deflation are disconnection from your spirit.

Chapter 3 Journaling

I feel most alive when...

My core values are...

What's worth giving my life energy to is...

The specific kinds of beauty that most inspire me are...

What I am grateful for is...

I am arrogant at times because...
The impact of my arrogance is...

I deflate myself at times because...
The impact of my self-deflation is...

Warm-up Questions

◆ Do I ever choose to be less than honest? Why?

◆ How clear are my agreements, and how consistent is my follow-through?

◆ In what sense is my relationship with my body a matter of integrity?

◆ Do I struggle with being a perfectionist? Or, on the other end of the spectrum, with being inattentive? Why?

~ Chapter Four ~

Integrity

INTEGRITY IS STANDING IN THE CENTER of your own truth. It is standing up for what you believe is right to think, say, or do. Imagine standing tall with your feet firmly planted and your spine straight. That's what Integrity looks and feels like. As a boy, my grandmother Mimi used to say to me, "Burke, stand up straight and look 'em in the eye." What made her words so powerful to my young spirit was that she said them with love—with a gleam in her eye that let me know she saw the strength in me and was inviting that potency into the world.

While the discipline of Integrity can be a space you feel lovingly invited into—a place to plant your feet on the ground, do your best to be true to yourself, be honest with others, and do what it takes to build a world that works—it can also be highly provocative. I know the sentiment in myself that sounds like, "question my love, question my intelligence, but don't question my integrity."

It's with this awareness—that Integrity can be both incredibly liberating and intensely challenging—that we wade into the deeper dimensions of Integrity as a discipline.

What Integrity is: being true
What Integrity does: sustains your life and relationships
Distortion: control
Repression: passiveness

PARADIGM SHIFT ALERT
From: Being in integrity means being limited or trapped by your ethics and commitments.
To: Being in integrity means being *bound* in order to be free. Being true to yourself and your commitments liberates you to more fully enjoy your life and have a positive impact on others.

Integrity sits in the west of the Medicine Wheel, opposite Inspiration. This positioning is symbolic of grounding our ideals and imagination in the tangible world. Integrity is intimately connected to Inspiration because it is aligning our actions with our sense of meaning and devotion. It is the discipline that enables us to have our own bodies, our experience of life, and the things we make and build in this world, match what we most deeply care about.

The discipline of Integrity is almost synonymous with *being accountable*. As you reflect on the creative practices of Integrity, you will see that a central theme woven throughout is the question of "who and what am I accountable to?"

In its essence, integrity is following through on your commitment to life, through your honesty, your devotion to excellence, and your willingness to tend to physical wellbeing, beginning with your own body and extending to the planet.

Integrity Archetypes: Warrior/Warrioress and Builder

The Warrior/Warrioress in you is the martial artist, committed to safeguarding life, not destroying it. It is the energy of impeccability of word and deed in the service of nobility. It is attending to balance in the physical realm. It is standing firmly for integrity in the system, whether that system is your body or your business team or your home or family.

The Builder in you is the one who creates structure, designs systems, and builds your world. It is the part of you that takes action in service of values and initiatives you believe in. It is your resolve, commitment, strength of will, and impeccable attention to detail and excellence.

Recall that archetypes are universally recognized energetic signatures. They represent a whole constellation of attitudes, skills, and ways of being with a particular genius to them.

Take a moment now to visualize and feel the Warrior/Warrioress and Builder in you—and the degrees to which you are familiar with them and have access to their particular energies.

The Core Practices of Integrity

Being Honest

Telling yourself the truth. Walking your talk. Honoring your commitments to yourself and others.

Bringing Excellence

Bringing you're A-game. Bringing structure, design, and high standards as essential elements of sustaining the quality of your life, work, and relationships.

Caring for Your Physical World

Treating the physical world, starting with your body and extending out to the planet, as sacred space—to be lived in with respect and care.

The Practice Elements

Being Honest

» Telling yourself the truth

» Being true to yourself and honest with others

» Making and keeping agreements

Bringing Excellence

» Attending to design and structure

» Embracing strictness

» Owning the expectations that drive you

Caring for Your Physical World

- » Living well in your body

- » Tending your ground

- » Sustaining Earth's natural systems

The Reactive Patterns of Integrity

Control

Passiveness

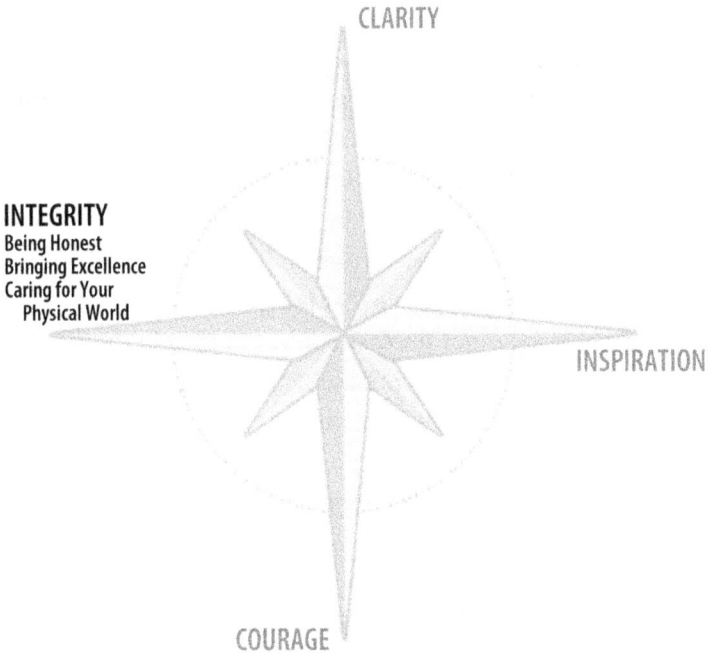

CLARITY

INTEGRITY
Being Honest
Bringing Excellence
Caring for Your
Physical World

INSPIRATION

COURAGE

Being Honest

"Let's be honest." Reflecting on how often we hear those words or find ourselves saying them, I've wondered why—and have come to believe it's partly because it feels good to be honest, and also because being honest is not always as easy as it sounds. As much as we would love to live in a world where we're either honest or not, where the truth is black and white, we just don't live in that world. We live in a world of many shades of gray, and we do our best to honor our sense of what is true in that world.

At a time in history—particularly on the political stage—where the notion of "alternative facts" has become a dangerous and eerily Orwellian excuse to promote in the public arena whatever version of reality one wants to believe, this notion of shades of gray is both tricky and essential. To navigate those shades requires that we demand from ourselves first, and then from others, a genuine commitment to seeking out what is true.

That's where the practice of honesty begins—with our desire to be true. As we honor that desire, we strengthen our credibility and our experience of respect, trust, and connection—and therefore find a power and influence that is authentic.

While honesty is not the easiest place to start in the discipline of Integrity, it is the most central. It is the key to being able to *live with ourselves* as well as live with others.

Honesty begins with telling ourselves the truth, then being true to ourselves, and third, being true to our agreements with others.

Telling Yourself the Truth

Being honest with yourself can begin with the easy stuff, like what you want or don't want, but quickly graduates to asking yourself the harder questions, like are you drinking too much alcohol, is your love relationship a healthy one, did you really want to be a parent, or are you happy in your job? To acknowledge the hard truths to yourself can be one of the most difficult and at the same time most freeing things you can do.

Why do we sometimes not tell ourselves the truth or acknowledge the facts of life as they present themselves? One possible reason is fear of upsetting the inner apple cart. If you know that you truly are in a job or a marriage that isn't right for you, you're faced with a disconnect that can be hard to live with. You may feel that your awareness demands action. It's important, however, to de-couple information from action. If you feel that you always have to act on what you sense is most true, being honest with yourself may feel just too demanding. It's important to know that you always have a choice of whether to act or not on your awareness of the truth. See your self-honesty as providing essential information. What you do with that information is a separate step from simply acknowledging it.

I once read, as graffiti on a men's room toilet stall of all places, "What are you pretending not to know?" While this might seem like a question about your knowing, it isn't primarily that. It's most essentially a question about your willingness. In other words, are you willing to admit to yourself a truth you already know, even if it's uncomfortable? To face what you know when it's uncomfortable takes activating a fierce aspect of yourself. The alternative—to be less than honest with yourself—may delay the discomfort, but often makes it worse when you finally do face the truth that has been nagging at you.

PARADIGM SHIFT ALERT
From: Being less than honest with yourself is some-times necessary to keep your life on an even keel and avoid regret, guilt, or things you'd rather not do or face. **To:** Being less than honest with yourself creates imbal-ance, self-sabotage, and often more pain in the long run.

One of the key places to look for the sometimes hard to dis-cover truth is in your actions. Often your actions are a very good indication of what is *actually*, versus theoretically, honest. Your ac-tions offer clues to what you truly believe, and who you really are. Notice the occasions when your actions deviate from your inten-tions. When that happens, rather than beating yourself up about it, take it as an opportunity to ask yourself why you didn't do what you intended. In that inquiry, you may discover something more about what's really true for you.

While your actions can inform you about your level of self-hon-esty, they can also build your self-honesty. In other words, if you act on something, rather than procrastinating or neglecting to fol-low through, you are being honest with yourself through the action you take, and you are building the muscle of self-honesty.

Being True to Yourself and Honest with Others

Being true to yourself—in other words being authentic—is the foundational ground of being true in the varied arenas of your life. In your relationships, your work, your social or religious communi-ties, your home environment, your physical health, and your rela-tionship with the planet itself. Being true to yourself is not selfish. It's the opposite. It is honoring your time here on Earth by contributing to the world in a way that is aligned with what you want to offer. It's one of the most obvious and powerful ways to embrace leadership as a way of bringing the gift of your fierce love to the world.

When you are consistently true to yourself, you liberate yourself to be true in all your relationships. Nelson Mandela was in prison for 28 years. On some very core essential level, all that time, he was free. That may sound crazy or naïve, but consider the possibility that he was free because he remained true to his core values, his purpose, and his humanity. He did not become someone other than he was. He maintained his integrity by being true to himself.

You may be tempted to think of that kind of integrity—aligning with your highest sense of yourself—as constraining, as too controlled. You may see it as keeping you from doing things you want to do. But consider letting go of the idea of integrity as *constraint*—and instead think of it as a *restraint* that liberates you. Restraint holds a freedom you are creating by being true to who you are at your best—drawing the line on what you believe is right for you to be and do.

It might seem that this concept of being free by being true to yourself is either too purist or too selfish. Perhaps you think there are times when being true to yourself is just not possible—like when you have to pay the bills, take care of the kids, and do the things at work that are annoying but have to be done anyway. These times are a reality of life for you and everyone. And perhaps your very normal struggles with them point not to a problem of being true to yourself, but to an opportunity to integrate in yourself what may seem like competing values.

A client who had moved his family to the US had to face a difficult reorganization affecting his job. He didn't like his options for staying, nor did he like the prospect of moving his family again. His value for satisfying work for himself seemed in direct opposition to his value for doing what was best for his family. Through deep reflection on what it could look like to honor both of his values, he was able to make a choice that he could not only live with, but thrive with.

There come times like this for most of us when we feel we have to decide between competing values. And there is tremendous truthfulness in that sense, because you are looking directly at your values, and attempting to balance, honor, and integrate different parts of yourself through your choices. Consider the perspective that your sincere effort to honor your various commitments in life—at times in opposition to each other—is being in Integrity.

Take the values of honesty and compassion for example. You may feel that saying what is really true for you will hurt someone else. Just your sincere grappling with these two values, and doing your best to honor them both, is being in integrity.

Your attempt to be true to yourself may at times feel like choosing between your own desires and values and the desires and values of others. Oriah Mountain Dreamer, in her book *The Invitation*, says "I want to know if you can disappoint another to be true to yourself, if you can bear the accusation of betrayal, and not betray your own soul." An invitation—perhaps at the edge of what any of us are able to consider—to walk the fine line of being responsible for the impact of our choices on others, while at the same time allowing others to be responsible for their own lives, choices, and ways they respond to us.

PARADIGM SHIFT ALERT
From: We have to choose between being true to ourselves or true to others.
To: Being true to ourselves enables us to be genuinely true, though not always pleasing, to others.

Sounding almost cold-hearted, and on the other hand potentially intensely respectful, these are certainly not small questions. Anyone who has divorced, or had an affair, or left a job, or walked away from a business deal, or moved away from family, or dropped a friendship, has struggled with being true to themselves while bearing the accusation of betrayal.

The critical mindset here is that being true to yourself is not at odds with being true to others. In fact, being true to yourself is essential to being true to others.

And yet, it is perfectly normal to be less than true to yourself, and therefore less than truthful with others. We often do this in an attempt to manage others' perceptions. And often for reasons that seem necessary for our wellbeing.

When we choose, however, to let go of managing others perceptions, and be true to ourselves in relationship, we are choosing a state of rawness and openness. As relationship expert and author Gay Hendricks says, the alternative to honesty is more like *entanglement* than relationship. The difference between relationship and entanglement is how honest we are about who we are, what we want, what we don't want, and our agenda. The fuller the self-disclosure, the cleaner and less entangled the relationship. When you are honest with others, they know who it is that they are in relationship with, and can make choices based on what's real. In that way, you aren't maintaining connection, peace, or approval by being less than genuine.

It's possible that being completely honest may have the impact of pain or upset in a relationship. How willing are you to experience that? Are there circumstances in which you should *not* risk that impact? How do you know whether to tell the truth or not? One way is to ask whether you are protecting yourself, holding up a false front, managing others perceptions of you, or avoiding conflict. Or are you (honestly) acting from a place of compassion and knowledge that complete honesty will serve no purpose and likely do harm? Try using these questions to inform the degree of honesty appropriate to a given situation.

To be honest in relationship demands an ability to come clean—to admit when and how you've betrayed your own sense of what's right, and then make it right again. The alternative is covering your ass.

One of the factors driving us to cover our ass is the feeling of shame, especially when it replaces what should be simply a feeling of guilt. Social researcher and psychologist Brené Brown says the difference between guilt and shame is that with guilt, you have *done something bad*; with shame, you *are bad*. So, if you believe that you *are* bad when you *do* bad, rather than simply feeling guilt, you may feel a shame that cuts too close to the core for comfort, inviting dishonesty about whatever you're feeling shame about. On the other hand, if you believe you are essentially whole, but also fallible, you can face guilt as a normal part of life.

When you carry shame, instead of cleanly dealing with guilt, you spend a lot of energy trying to prove yourself, fix yourself, make up for your deficiency, and sometimes covering up for it. It's a waste. Let's just admit we are all imperfect, and get on with the business of doing our best, and owning up to it when we don't.

Making and Keeping Agreements

A hallmark of integrity is making agreements—with yourself as well as with others—that you can keep. When you make and keep agreements, you build your trustworthiness. You also create a guidance system for your actions. Consider that almost everything you do is delivering on some form of agreement—whether it's a promise you make to yourself about adopting a healthier diet, or a commitment you make to your boss to deliver a project on time.

When you make agreements consciously, intentionally, and

with a sense of excitement and awareness of the power they con-
tain—your life takes on an energy of direction and achievement.
Every time you keep a commitment, you consciously or unconsciously strengthen the trust in your relationship with yourself
and/or with someone else.

One of the most pervasive and yet often overlooked examples
of an agreement we make with one another is that of time. Yes,
time is actually an agreement to honor one of the most precious
things we each have. My grandmother once said to me, "Burke,
when you're late, you are breaking one of the Ten Commandments."
I was a bit shocked, but she had my attention. "How so?" I said.
"When you show up late to meet with someone, you are stealing
their time." I've never forgotten that. It doesn't mean that I always
show up on time now, but I do much better than I used to, and am
much more aware of the impact of being late to an appointment.

You make agreements with others about time, and you also
make agreements about time with yourself. Your choices of how
to spend your time are key indicators of your integrity. Your relationship with time is a measure of how you honor your values and
highest intentions. Your effectiveness at creating the experience of
life that you want is directly connected to the choices you make
around time. To make good use of your time takes a *fierce-love* kind
of discipline—fiercely loving your life, and defending its most precious resource.

While making and keeping agreements may sometimes feel
confining, the reality is just the opposite. Promises are incredibly
freeing—because following through on commitments paves the
way to having what you want. Achieving any goal, or building any
relationship, is a direct result of keeping the promises it took to get
there.

Where it gets most challenging—and perhaps most exciting and growth-propelling—is when you find that you can't keep an agreement—either before it's broken, or after. When you know you can't keep a promise you've made, and you renegotiate before you break it, you build your integrity. When you break an agreement without renegotiating first, it's what you do next that reveals the strength of your honesty.

One of the ways you reveal your integrity is looking at the degree to which you have dropped excuse-making from your thinking and your language. There are always reasons for not being true to yourself, or not keeping your agreements with others. Always. But what if you made those reasons/excuses irrelevant? What if, instead of making excuses, you simply acknowledged the breakdown, and renewed or renegotiated your commitment?

And if you do explain your reason for breaking a commitment, ask yourself what your explanation is in the service of. Are you serving the other person by giving them important information? Or, does your explanation have a flavor of letting yourself off the hook, justifying your actions, or playing the victim card? If any of those are true, it's best to drop it. Just acknowledge the breakdown, however large or small, do what's possible to clean it up, and move on with a renewed or renegotiated agreement.

- What am I pretending not to know? Why? What's the impact?
- What agreement have I made—with myself or another—that I need to more impeccably follow through on?

Bringing Excellence

Bring your A-game is the mantra of excellence. When you bring your A-game—when you bring excellence—you honor something in you that knows, as Marianne Williamson says, how "brilliant, gorgeous, talented and fabulous" you are. Not because you need to prove yourself, but because it feels good to bring the best of yourself to the many aspects of your life.

Excellence is inspiration made tangible. It is the precise and exacting follow through on what you feel called to do. Excellence, while *sourced by* your inspiration, is also a *source of* inspiration. Consider the Olympic Games, space travel, world-class ballet, and some of your own accomplishments.

Excellence is as much a way of thinking as it is an outcome. It is an orientation toward life that says "if I'm here on the planet, let me go for it. Let me not settle for mediocrity, but do my best in all that I do." Again, not because mediocrity is wrong or bad. But because excellence is more creative—more generative of what you want for this one amazing life that you have.

Bringing excellence is most connected to Integrity when it comes from an internal excitement about operating at the highest level you can. It is less in integrity when you are motivated by fear of looking bad, or are driven by a need for external validation. To bring excellence means to be impeccable without having to be perfect. Its medicine is strongest when it is less a taskmaster and more an enabler.

Excellence is how we create the world we can imagine. When you think of products that inspire you rather than simply meet your needs, what you are often responding to is excellence. When you think of the work you have been most proud of, what you are often acknowledging is your willingness to bring excellence.

PARADIGM SHIFT ALERT
From: Excellence is a taskmaster.
To: Excellence is an enabler.

While excellence at times requires more effort than mediocrity, most often it simply requires more attentiveness. For example, it takes hardly more effort to get the dishes really clean than getting them somewhat clean. Or to make an exceptional business pitch versus a passable one.

So much of what works in our lives is directly connected to excellence and precision. Your car is dependable because of it. Food is on the grocery shelves because of it. Your kitchen faucet works because people held themselves to high standards of excellence.

Attending to Design and Structure

Design and structure are the backbone of excellence. Without being well-designed and well made, much of what we count on in life would fall apart. Structure literally holds your life together—your home, your relationships, your professional contribution.

For example, creating effective organizational decision-making processes; running effective meetings; aligning financial compensation with strategic priorities; and setting up office space and furniture that foster productivity.

The quality of your relationships also benefits from design and structure. Organizational roles and responsibilities are an example of design that enhances relationship. So are date nights.

At home, attention to design versus being haphazard, is essential to creating a physical environment that nurtures the best in you. The Chinese have known this for centuries, and long practiced the art of Feng Shui as a means of enhancing the creative flow of life energy through architectural and spatial design.

Bringing thoughtful organization to your office, closet, kitchen—you name it—is more than a nice-to-have. It's a matter of integrity. For some people, that's an obvious statement. For others, a very challenging one. I'm in the latter category. It's taken years, and a patient and persistent spouse, to help me get there—to help me appreciate that being organized is not a blight on my spontaneity. It supports, rather than detracts from, the experience of life and work that I want to have.

In the arena of personal relationships, you can apply all of these aspects of design to a marriage or parenting—shared core values and norms, fairness, consistent messaging, and setting an example. They support your life in much the same way as foundation walls and I-beams hold up a building's roof.

PARADIGM SHIFT ALERT
From: Structure kills spontaneity.
To: Structure makes spontaneity more generative and rewarding.

Especially consider the essential nature of structure in any change process. Innovation—whether personal or organizational—requires structure to support new habits. You start with an idea to change something—a manufacturing process, office protocol, or your physical fitness routine. Your idea becomes an intention, and then requires a structure to see it through.

The integrity in attending to design and structure is the degree to which it supports your highest intentions. In business, for example, the integrity of processes, events, roll-outs, and communications depend on the way you structure them to support your intended impact. In maintaining your health and fitness, the integrity of your diet and physical exercise regimen is the degree to which their design supports the state of wellness you want to achieve.

Kahlil Gibran, in *The Prophet*, wrote, "Work is love made visible." It may also be true that work is integrity made visible. When you take your love and your passion, and support them with your integrity, with good design and structure, you get excellent work in the world.

Embracing Strictness

When we set up strict rules to govern ourselves individually, and laws to govern ourselves collectively, are we limiting our ability to fully express ourselves in life and community, or enabling and enhancing that expression? Of course, as with any paradox, the answer is yes and yes. It's both—embracing the paradoxical notion of *strictness that liberates*. And particularly, in this context, liberates excellence.

Anyone who has mastered a skill knows that excellence in most endeavors must include strictly embracing certain rules or laws. Think of art, music, or mathematics. Being firmly grounded in the basic principles that underpin a discipline is essential to any level of mastery.

There is something liberating, and honoring of your integrity, to consciously agree to, and acknowledge, the every-day rules that govern how we move and relate in the world. When you willingly, versus reluctantly, choose to embrace and honor the laws of your world—whether societal or physical—you shift from being a begrudging follower to being an appreciator of strictness as essential to effectively navigating life.

In addition to the laws of society or an established discipline, there are the rules you lay down for yourself. These are essential to a life of excellence. It's actually quite liberating to make a strict guideline for yourself, especially if it's in support of a habit you want to maintain. For example, if you want to stay fit, and you make a rule to work out three times a week, no exceptions, you are much more likely to actually work out, than if you leave the decision up to how you feel each week.

The usefulness of strictness to enable excellence is equal to the consciousness we bring to our relationship with the rules we create. Meaning, our ability to achieve excellence depends largely on our ability to continually assess whether the rules, systems and structures we've created are still useful in helping us to create the best world (products, relationships, families, etc) we can imagine. When rules or laws don't empower us, it's time to challenge them—and less from a mindset of rebellion, and more from a mindset of commitment to excellence and being true to the impulses of creative expression and evolution as human beings. Without the option to challenge and change the laws, rules, and principles we live by when our highest visions call for it, there would be very little innovation or progress in the world.

Owning the Expectations that Drive You

Excellence as a practice of Integrity is most powerful when seen as a calling to live *into*, more than a standard to live *up to*. The distinction is one of responding to internal drivers and inspirations versus external obligations or tests.

Excellence as a response to what inspires you, and to a felt sense of the capabilities, potential, talent and desires that live inside you, can be the adventure of a lifetime—exciting, fun, even exhilarating. But for that to be true means listening more to what's inside than what's outside—to self-expectation intimately sensed and freely chosen. Which means you own it. While your family, your company, your culture, or your religion are legitimate influences, it's ultimately not up to them to tell you what excellence looks like in your life, or what should drive it. You can respond to provocations from all those places. But the excellence that calls you is most powerful and creative when it comes from inside.

In every client engagement, we do some version of recalibrating the expectations of excellence they are responding to in their lives. Occasionally this means a complete change in career. In other cases, it is simply a shift to being more driven by their internal sense of purpose and less by the expectations of others.

One client, after more than a decade of working as a marketing executive, decided to move into the human services field, and now runs a shelter for the homeless in a major city. Another decided to step out of his family business to lead an organization more in line with his passion and purpose. While these are big life-trajectory examples, there are many smaller opportunities every day. Whether in a large or small context, the point is to recognize and be willing to follow an internal calling instead of an external obligation— matched by a courageous commitment to honor those callings to bring excellence.

This does not mean there's no place for being driven by external expectations. Of course there is. When you sign up for a role in an organization, a team, even a family, there are expectations you commit to meeting. You agree to be part of creating and delivering on those expectations. The key is to explicitly choose in. To choose and communicate what you say yes to and no to.

You empower yourself and others around you when you consciously and clearly choose, versus passively accept, the expectations you take on, even in small ways. What happens when you are given a task—whether it's to lead a new product launch or to pick up your child's birthday cake—and you take it on as yours? Not someone else's bequest to fulfill, but your task to own. As soon as you say yes to a request, if you own it, and commit yourself to deliver on it at the highest level you can, it becomes yours.

PARADIGM SHIFT ALERT
From: Integrity is delivering on the expectations of others.
To: Integrity is owning the expectations that drive you as yours, including when they initially come from others. While you may honor the bars others set for you, ultimately it is you who sets and goes after your own high bars.

But what happens when someone else's idea of who you should be, or what you should do, clashes with what you expect of yourself? Ideally, you make it a conversation that honors both you and the other, and that leads to your yes or no being aligned with your highest intentions for both self-honoring and honoring someone else.

The realization that you are always in charge of the expectations you live into—by choosing to say yes or no—frees you from the idea that you have no choice but to climb mountains or reach for bars that others set for you. It instead helps you see that no one gets you into something. Only you do. With the exception of blatantly coercive circumstances, we are the ones who get ourselves into things. When you acknowledge that you are responsible for your choice to say yes or no, you own the expectations in your life. From a place of ownership, delivering on those expectations builds self-respect and enhances the quality of your experience.

ACTIVATION QUESTIONS
- In what form is excellence called for in my life right now?
- What am I saying yes to, and no to? How is that empowering or disempowering me?

Caring for Your Physical World

It's easy to forget that we are physical bodies in a physical world. To take that fact for granted, or to fail to honor it, is to be in less than full integrity with ourselves and our world. Mastering Integrity must include an intimate relationship with our physical environment and bodily existence.

Living Well in Your Body

Most people relate to their bodies as a mere vehicle to use, rather than a wondrous and complex ecosystem to live well in. Instead of actually living in our bodies, we tend to live in our heads, and use our bodies as vehicles to move our heads around from place to place. There's a big difference between *living in* your body, and *using* your body. When you use your body, you're happy with it when it looks good enough to be attractive, and when it's healthy enough to keep you doing whatever it is you do. As long as our bodies are working well, they're mostly off our radar screens. As long as our bodies *perform*, we get along with them just fine. We often treat our bodies as things to use, abuse, and fix, rather than to live intimately in.

Living well in your body is a vast topic which whole industries have grown up around—some more honoring of real health in the body than others. What feels most honoring to me is to start with a mindset of the body as sacred—an ecosystem or temple (pick your metaphor) to respect and steward.

I want to offer four areas of focus for living more intimately in your own body as sacred—performance, pleasure, listening, and impact.

Your body is the biological system that is your home, no matter where you are. That living system has certain requirements for optimal vibrancy. Enough water. The right quality of nutrients. Physical activity that matches your particular constitution and sensibilities—whether it's dance, skiing, yoga, walking, or ultra-marathon-running. When your body is a temple to inhabit, you're less likely to put "trash" (like junk food) in it. You're less likely to take your body for granted. You're less likely to abuse it—whether through too little sleep, too much sitting, or sex that doesn't feel right for you.

PARADIGM SHIFT ALERT
From: Your body is a vehicle to carry your head from place to place.
To: Your body is a sacred ecosystem, or to use another metaphor—a temple—to be lived in and honored, rather than a vehicle to be used.

When most people begin to consider living well in their bodies, they think primarily of performance—whether that means looking good, carrying out daily activities with more ease and less pain, or excelling in sport. Beyond performance though, and equally important, is pleasure. Your body is built for pleasure, and responding to that design plays a key role in creating the wholeness in your body that is an essential aspect of Integrity. The pleasure of living in your body is primarily through sensory awareness—the taste of food, the feel of a warm ocean breeze on your skin, and a loved-one's hand in yours—so many varied sensory pleasures available to us when we're paying attention to them.

Ideally, living well in your body combines pleasure and performance. Take your diet for instance. Notice the foods that are not only healthy but taste great in your mouth. Or sport—my favorite is snow skiing—the pleasure of sun on my face, views of majestic mountain ranges, spruce and aspen, and the feel of grace and rhythm—is exquisite to me. My other sport-love is swimming. And not just to get a workout. I love the feel of the water enveloping my body, and the way my hand slices into it. The more you make performance also a matter of pleasure, rather than struggle, the easier it is to sustain the activities that truly honor your body.

Third, to live well in your body is a practice of listening—in three ways—listening to your body, listening to what you are saying to your body, and listening with your body to the world around you.

Listening to your body is the best way to know what it needs in order to be vibrantly alive. But all too often, for most people, our bodies speak to us, and we essentially say "shut up and take some drugs." What if we instead listened more carefully, and paid attention? Imagine the ripple effects on fitness, preventative care, productivity, and enjoying life.

You'll be surprised how much your body has to say when you

take quiet moments to tune into it. One way is to do a body scan. From one end to the other, put your attention on all the areas of your body. Ask each area what it needs from you. Or, simply ask your body in general what it needs, and see what area of the body your attention is drawn to.

It's amazing how much wisdom your body holds. If you listen, it will give you information not only about what it needs, but what is good for your whole being in general. If you're making an important decision, ask your gut what it knows about the choice in front of you. Listen to the thoughts that come.

As much as your body is speaking to you, you are also speaking to it, and your listening can help you know what messages your body needs to hear. You are sending messages to your body all the time through lifestyle choices (diet, exercise, etc). You are also sending messages through your thoughts. The next time you look in the mirror, notice what you are thinking, and what kind of messages your thoughts are sending to your body. The next time you go for a workout, notice whether you are taking your body to the gym to *get it in shape*, or to *nourish it*. Your actions and thoughts send to your body messages of appreciation and care, or of judgment, neglect, or abuse. Whatever the messages are, your body absorbs them, and responds accordingly. Just as a child absorbs messages from parents about worth, your body takes its cues about its value from the messages you send through your actions, choices and thoughts—and your body responds with either enhanced or diminished vibrancy.

A third way of bodily listening is to listen *with* your body. To more consciously turn on, and more acutely tune into, your senses—to be in direct sensual relationship with life—to actually hear the birds and the wind in the trees; to see the lines and texture in buildings and notice the movement of waves on water; to notice the smells in your environment and really taste the coffee in your cup. Turning on your senses is a sign of deep respect and appreciation for your body and the way it connects you to your life. When you practice yoga, martial arts, dance, sacred sexuality, or other activities that involve acute body-awareness, you are honoring life directly by listening to how your own body responds to it. This is an expression of integrity that has a profound effect on the quality of your experience.

Lastly, the fourth key aspect of living well in your body is paying attention to its impact. Notice how you are inhabiting and holding your body, and the impact it has on you and the people around you. Notice your posture and your body language. Are you upright, slouched, rigid, relaxed but strong? These aspects of being in your body impact how you feel about yourself. They also impact how others feel about you and feel about themselves in your presence—primarily in two ways, attraction and inspiration. As human beings, we are more open to things—and people—we are attracted to. When you carry yourself with confidence, or with ease, or alertness, you become more attractive. This tends to make people more comfortable in your presence, and more open to you. It can also inspire them by conveying an energy that reminds them of their most powerfully embodied self.

In addition to your posture and how you hold yourself, paying attention to the impact of your body extends to the clothes you wear. For most of my life, I thought almost solely in terms of dressing casually and comfortably. Until I met my wife. She taught me to see clothes through a lens of "dressing one's soul." It's the concept of matching the quality and energy of the clothes you wear with the qualities of the human being inside them. This is not worn-out truisms like dress for success, or dress to impress others, but more about dress to honor. It's less about having the latest fashions or the most expensive brand names, and more about wearing clothes that fit—not just fit your body, but who you are on the inside.

The way you inhabit and hold your body, from your level of fitness to the way you dress, sends a message to those around you. There's no right message to send, but there is an opportunity to be more conscious and intentional about it. Not so that you can pose and impress, but so that you can, with your authentic care, convey who you are and what you value, and inspire others to have a similar honoring relationship with their own bodies.

Tending Your Ground

An extension of living well in your body, and a way of further honoring your physical world, is tending your ground. This means looking at the ways that your physical world—how you relate to it, and how you have set it up—creates the ground, or support structures, for your physical wellbeing.

There are many ways of tending to the support structures of your life. Taking care of your finances is one. Money is a gigantic player in the practice of honoring your physical existence. It's important to look at your relationship to money through that lens. Ask yourself whether you are managing your money well. Are you giving it the right kind of attention? Is it supporting not only your physical wellbeing, but your ability to align with your core values?

Another big way to tend the ground of your physical wellbeing is to really pay attention to the quality of your home and work environments, and to the ways you're relating to them. For example, you hear it often said these days that "sitting is the new smoking." I have put a stand-up desk in my office to enable me to stand and walk around while I talk with clients, and still be able to take notes on my computer.

A client who was directing the creative work for a marketing campaign for a major US company found herself working in an office that was cold and sterile. It had a visceral impact that made it much more challenging for her and others to be creatively productive in that environment. She found herself getting very innovative with the furniture, art, and arrangement of space—in the name of honoring the physicality of her workplace and its impact on the teams occupying it.

In my thirties, I researched and wrote articles for *Solar Today Magazine* on the technologies and health benefits of office buildings and schools that took optimal advantage of natural daylight. Since that time we've seen increasingly compelling evidence that daylighting (as the design approach is called) improves concentration, reduces eyestrain, and improves our overall sense of wellbeing.

When it comes to the human-built environment and the things we use every day, to varying degrees in our society we've paid increasing attention over the years to the levels of toxicity we expose ourselves to. This attention and the corrective actions we take is a way of tending our ground. Consider the couch you're sitting on as you read this book, or the air you're breathing, or the frying pan you made your eggs in this morning.

PARADIGM SHIFT ALERT
From: Caring for our bodies and caring for our environments are two separate things.
To: Caring for our bodies and the environments we inhabit are inextricably interconnected.

When it comes to the world of nature around us, there is an additional opportunity to tend your ground by putting your body in contact with the natural world in ways that nourish you. Your body, in a very literal sense, is nature in human form. The more contact you have with nature, the healthier it is for you. Standing or walking barefoot on the ground, for instance, allows you to connect with the particular vibration of the earth, which uniquely supports health in your body. Walking in nature with no particular agenda—allowing your eyes to engage with a wide range of distances, colors, and patterns; exposing your lungs to fresh air; asking your ears and brain to take in and process a variety of sounds—this is a way of tending the ground of your physical being. Our bodies are more like animal bodies than most of us realize—we honor that reality by increasing the presence of nature in our daily experience.

In the more domestic arena, gardening, caring for animals, being with your dog or cat, are also ways of tending the ground. Even simple things like watering your house plants, splitting wood for your fireplace, or fixing a healthy meal, honor your body's need to engage with and be supported by the physical world you live in.

Sustaining Earth's Natural Systems

Years ago, fresh out of college, I read the book *Person/Planet*, by Theodore Roszak. It brought my awareness to a way of seeing the world, and thinking about life, that has never left me. Roszak described the many ways that what creates true health in the human being is also good for the planet. And vice versa—that when we live in ways that diminish our wholeness, we also harm the planet. His thesis was an early articulation of a field of study that married ecology and psychology, and became known as ecopsychology.

Your body is a microcosm of the planet. A few minutes of reflection will lead you to the same conclusion. Consider the percentage of your body—and the percentage of the planet's surface—that is comprised of water. Consider the minerals and atomic structures of both your body and life on planet Earth. Or the flow of energy from the sun that enlivens both your own biology and that of the planet's ecosystems.

As a young man in my early thirties, I moved to Colorado—

initially to study solar energy technologies as a practical contribution to living in ways that helped sustain rather than deplete the natural systems of the planet. In the process, I had the privilege of interning with Amory Lovins at the Rocky Mountain Institute. And meeting Paul Hawken, co-founder of Smith and Hawken and author of *The Ecology of Commerce*. On a beautiful summer day in Snowmass, walking with Paul on the Windstar Foundation land, we talked about the future of the environmental movement. Paul's perspective powerfully resonated with me—that environmental progress would not occur through seeing people as a blight on the planet, or through scarcity and deprivation mindsets. Our best hope to make progress was to capitalize on human motivation and ingenuity to create products and services that made our lives richer, not more austere. Paul saw abundant living for people and the health of the planet as complementary goals rather than a zero-sum game.

Paul's view, which has been echoed and expanded by progressive economists and ecologists for several decades now, is an underlying motivation for doing the work I do with corporate leaders. I am convinced that the key to living well on the planet lies in our resolve and ability to engage in commerce in ways that holds human well-being and the health of the planet as inextricably intertwined.

More and more we see this point of view articulated by prominent corporate leaders like Howard Schultz, former CEO of Starbucks, John Mackey of Whole Foods, in his book *Conscious Business*, and Bruno Roche of Mars in his book *Completing Capitalism*.

From: Sustaining people and sustaining Earth's natural systems are at odds. In other words, to protect the planet means to neglect people.

To: Commerce not only can, but must, contribute to the physical wellbeing of people while also sustaining and restoring the health of the planet.

My view—more accurately, my stand—is that the mindset of corporate social and environmental sustainability is essential, not peripheral, to leadership. And that it is a necessary, not optional, defining characteristic of Integrity. At the same time, I'm under no illusion that this is easy. The card deck of conventional economics and political policy is stacked against it. To create ways of doing business that are as much restorative as depleting of the planet's ecosystems, and honor contributions more fairly across the social spectrum, requires—like all expressions of responsibility—awareness, intention, and choice. And to make choices that fly against convention requires resolve and will. Which by the way, there is much of in the corporate world. The question is how that resolve will be channeled.

A related mindset holds that our approach to economics on the macro level is intertwined with, and therefore must be mirrored by, the way we live as individuals. In other words, contributing to the wellbeing of the planet by caring for the health of its natural systems is deeply personal—starting with living in your own body as a sacred ecosystem, and extending to things like spending your money on environmentally and socially responsible products and services.

This brings us full circle. Honoring your personal ecology starts with your body but doesn't stop there. It extends to the environ-ments you live and work in, and beyond to the planet. Treat your body as you would the planet. Or treat the planet as you would your body. It doesn't matter where you start. What matters is that you create a cycle of reciprocity, emerging from a sense of intercon-nectedness.

Translating philosophy into application in this arena is most centrally a matter of asking yourself to what degree you are hon-oring your own body and the planet at the same time. And then acting on the answers you get.

ACTIVATION QUESTIONS
- How am I listening *to* my body and *with* my body?
- What am I saying *to* my body and *with* my body?

Control and Passiveness

(The Reactive Patterns of Integrity)

Integrity is uprightness (backbone, strength, being honest with yourself and others, upholding high standards of excellence, and honoring the physicality of life).

Control—the distortion of Integrity—is being self-righteous (ver-sus upright), and attempting to make yourself and/or others fit your idea of how one should live or do things, sometimes through bullying or brow-beating.

Passiveness—the repression of integrity—is not caring, taking your eye off the ball, and sometimes passively manipulating others to pick it up.

Control has a tight, white-knuckled energy. Passiveness has a lax hands-off energy. Integrity, in contrast, has an energy of relaxed intensity. Metaphorically, Integrity is a warm firm handshake; control is a vice-grip; and passiveness is a limp fish handshake.

Integrity is to align your actions with your highest intentions. Control and passiveness are ways to manipulate—forcefully or passively—life circumstances, others, and yourself to *get in line*.

Remember, as you read about control and passiveness, that we all are subject to reactivity from time to time through lack of awareness and intention. The inner adventure is to catch ourselves in reaction, and in the spirit of radical responsibility, choose the Discipline over the distortion or repression.

Control (Integrity Distorted)

The ballgame on TV goes to commercial. Music starts, and a sleek European luxury sedan pulls up to a stone mansion in the lush countryside; the suave male voice-over declares "control is power." This is the prevailing way of thinking—the more control we have, the more power we have.

In one sense, it is true. Control *is* power. When you put your attention on what you can control—in other words, on how you show up—you are exercising your personal power in a healthy way. You are actually being in integrity. But control as a bullying or dictatorial stance toward life and other people, is a distortion of Integrity, and a life-diminishing expression of power.

A simple distinction between Integrity and control is the difference between *exercising your will in* the world, versus *forcing your will on* the world. Integrity is forming yourself to your ideals, whereas control is trying to force the world to conform to your ideas. Integrity is focused on the way you are showing up in the world, rather than making the world look the way you think it should.

One of the ways we try to control life and people is through perfectionism—which can be confused with excellence. Perfectionism, as distinct from excellence, is a form of aggression that can be downright violent, hurting yourself as much as it hurts others. You can brow-beat yourself in order to maintain your perfectionism as much as you can brow-beat another person to live up to your standards.

Rather than perfectionism, Integrity is paying attention to where excellence is called for in life, and making choices about the bar you set for yourself and others. The invitation is to appreciate excellence where you encounter it, making room for (even appreciating) imperfection, and setting your sights high—all at the same time.

How do you strike a balance between excellence and perfectionism? Ask yourself if your attention to excellence feels liberating and enjoyable, or if it feels suffocating—and take that as your feedback and guide to a healthy balance.

Micromanagement can be a particularly damaging form of perfectionism. It is insisting on having your way. It is leading as an autocrat. It is being bossy, bending others to your will. It can be a form of aggression, even violence, as it disrespects others' autonomy and value.

Turned inward, perfectionism is being overly driven, overly independent, and cracking the whip on yourself in a way that is harmful to your spirit. In it's extreme, perfectionism turned inward is obsessive compulsive behavior. Turned outward, it's a type of aggression.

All of that said, given the bullying nature of perfectionism, whether turned inward or outward, it's important to understand that perfectionism is a reaction to fear. A perfectionist, or someone who micromanages, is almost never intending to be a controlling asshole. Almost always, they are acting out of their own fear and mistrust. So it helps when confronted with a micromanager or perfectionist, or with those tendencies in yourself, to get curious about the fears, and do what you can to allay them, rather than try to oust the perfectionist in you.

PARADIGM SHIFT ALERT
From: Perfectionism is a badge of honor.
To: Perfectionism is a brand of bullying—whether it's turned on yourself, or inflicted on others.

Passiveness (Integrity Repressed)

In contrast to control, which can sound like "I've got this, and I'm the only one who can get this, and by the way it's my way or the highway," passiveness is the opposite—a kind of helplessness. In relationship, passiveness is neglect and inattention. It is unconsciously attempting to manipulate others through being overly needy or indirect. Turned inward on yourself, passiveness is both self-indulgence and self-neglect, neither of which are aligning your actions with your highest intentions. In contrast to control, which is being too rigid, passiveness is being too lax. It is a kind of laziness, the other side of the coin from over-drive.

Just as much as over control diminishes your results and experience of life, passiveness can also destroy your dreams and intentions—letting you down, and others down.

ACTIVATION QUESTIONS
• Is there anything I am micromanaging?
• Is there something I am neglecting that I really want to pay attention to?

Chapter 4 Summary Points

Integrity is aligning with your devotion to Life and respect for yourself in a way that creates ground under your feet. To do anything else—to be dishonest, or do shoddy work, or neglect what supports your physical life—all put you on shifting sands rather than firm ground.

Being Honest

Honesty with yourself frees you to be yourself and be authentic in relationship. Your honesty comes out as much in your actions as in your words. You might be dishonest with yourself when, 1) it's uncomfortable to face your flaws, or 2) you don't want to rock the boat in your life circumstances or in relationship.

Honesty with yourself enables you to be true to yourself, rather than sell your soul. This becomes particularly poignant and transformational when it means disappointing others.

Honesty with others frees you to have a real relationship, versus an entanglement. Others get to be in relationship with the real *you*, rather than a façade you're maintaining.

Essential expressions of honesty include fully owning what you say yes and no to, making and keeping clear agreements, and ditching excuse-making.

Bringing Excellence

Excellence is holding the world in high regard by giving your best to it. Excellence is a mindset, as much as it is a description of high quality. When you look through the mindset of excellence, you honor possibility.

Excellence is what makes your life work—in everything from how you design business systems, to how you spend your time, to the quality of your conversations. In going for excellence, structure and rules are essential allies—until they limit you.

Excellence arises in consciously saying yes to your capability, and to the expectations you choose to deliver on.

Caring for your Physical World
Respect your body as a sacred living system that you are at home in, that you listen to, and that you nourish with appreciation and care. Do what is needed to create environments that support your physical wellbeing, and to contribute to the health of the planet while honoring the quality of your own physical life.

Control and Passiveness
Control is the distortion of Integrity because while it may come from the same impulse to uphold excellence, it does so through perfectionistic or bullying behavior. Passiveness is the repression of integrity because it neglects what it takes—the honesty, will, and commitment—to build a life that works.

Chapter 4 Journaling

A time I have been out of integrity was:

>> I was thinking...

>> I was feeling...

>> The cost was...

>> I learned...

I sometimes lie to myself about...

I know I am "selling out" when...

I cover my ass when.... Because...

The ways that structure in my life liberates me are...

The ways I treat my body as sacred are...

I am controlling when... The impact is....

I am passive about... The impact is...

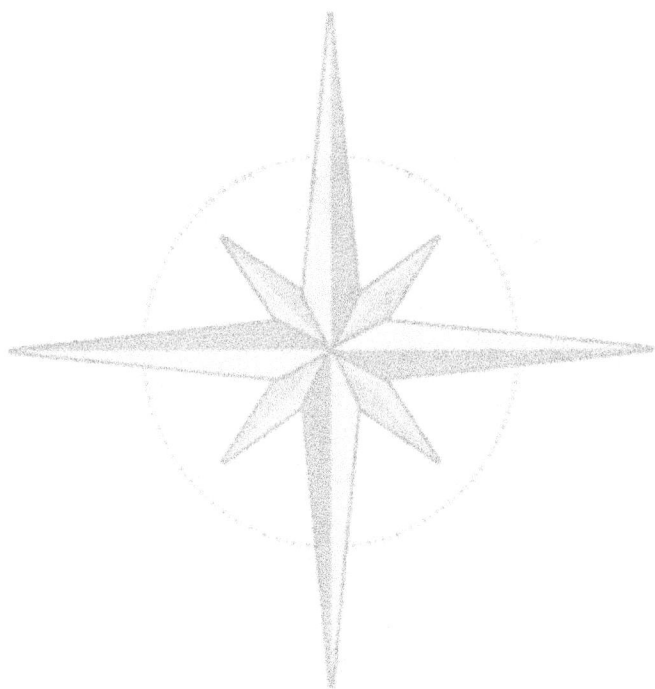

Warm-up Questions

- What does it mean to me to be wholehearted?

- To what degree do I let myself be seen and felt by others?

- How willing am I to forgive myself, or someone else?

- When I feel criticized, judged, or unfairly blamed, do I tend to get defensive or rather to emotionally withdraw?

Courage

THE WORD COURAGE is derived from the Latin word *cor*, and the French *coeur*, meaning heart. Courage is being present in the world with your heart open and fully engaged. It is showing up wholeheartedly for life, whatever that brings.

What Courage is: being wholehearted
What it does: strengthens emotional presence
Distortion: defensiveness
Repression: withdrawal

PARADIGM SHIFT ALERT
From: Courage is being impervious to fear, discomfort, and emotional pain.
To: Courage is being willing to experience everything in life, including fear and pain, with your heart open and available.

Courage is not about being unafraid. Courage is being emotionally available—to everything, including fear. It is meeting the pains and joys of life with a strong, loving heart, not an impervious one. It is living with an open-hearted sense of adventure.

Courage Archetypes: Lover and Adventurer

The Lover in you is the one who lives in a state of deep appreciation—for yourself, for others, and for the many ways that life presents itself to you. The lover in you extends compassion and kindness out into the world, even with people and situations that feel hard to love, and even when you've been hurt before.

The Adventurer in you is the one who takes emotional risks, and is courageous in the face of your own fear. Your adventurer is not faint of heart, and does not withdraw from life when it's painful, but keeps opening to possibilities and opportunities.

Recall that archetypes are universally recognized energetic signatures. They represent a whole constellation of attitudes, skills, and ways of being with a particular genius to them.

Take a moment now to visualize and feel the Lover and Adventurer in you—and the degrees to which you are familiar with them and have access to their particular energies.

The Core Practices of Courage

Leaning In

Keeping your heart open to the presence of emotion in yourself and in those around you. Allowing emotion to move you, inform you, and grow you.

Braving Connection

To brave the intimacy of connection is both vulnerable and empathetic. It is choosing your own emotional exposure, risk, and openness while also tuning into the experience of others. One of the deepest levels of connection is a willingness and ability to let go.

Living in Appreciation

Finding and actively acknowledging the good in yourself, others, and your world. The more challenging life is, the more difficult—and the more powerful—it is to harness appreciation.

The Practice Elements

Leaning In

- » Being emotionally aware and available

- » Listening to emotion

- » Navigating discomfort and upset

Braving Connection

- » Seeing and being seen

- » Choosing trust

- » Letting go

Living in Appreciation

- » Being a person of increase
- » Appreciating the hard stuff
- » Forgiving

The Reactive Patterns of Courage

Defensiveness

Withdrawal

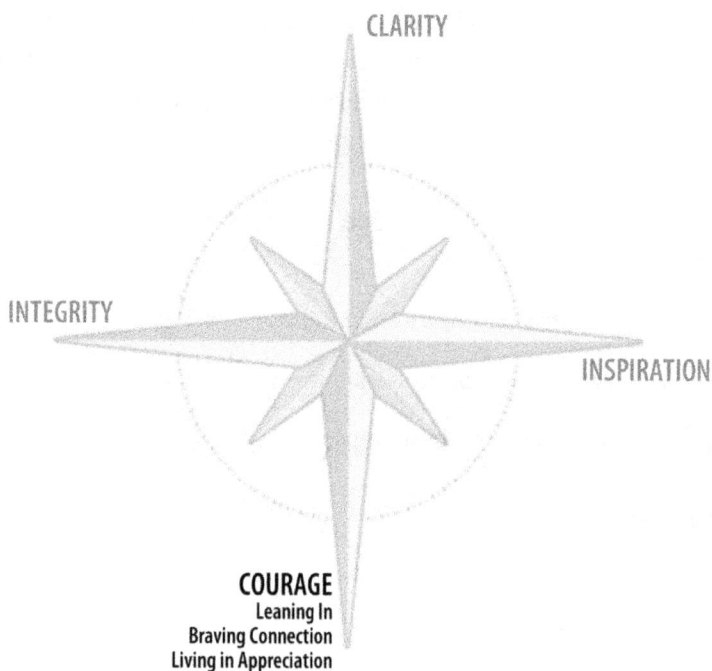

Leaning In

I was sitting in Omaha, Nebraska with an executive team when one of the leaders took a leap of courage and addressed an elephant in the room—an issue everyone knew was holding the team back, but no one was willing to talk about. It wasn't a comfortable moment, but it was a watershed one. His willingness to press through his own discomfort emboldened the team to engage in other courageous conversations and create a new norm for candid discussion.

In that team session, big issues got addressed. Yet perhaps even more exciting to me was the learning—that being courageous enough to address an emotionally-charged issue does the exact opposite of what team members were afraid it would do. Rather than cause a breakdown in relationships, it created a breakthrough—resulting in greater trust and stronger connections. Reflecting on the breakthrough, the team discovered a leadership principle they named as "when it's scary, lean in."

Leaning in is essential to having tough conversations. And it's more than that. It is essential to having the life and impact you want to have. Leaning in means opening your heart to the adventure of life, especially when your fear tells you to keep your heart small and unexposed.

Leaning in is a practice of being in healthy relationship with your emotions and the emotions you encounter in others. Its three core elements are being emotionally aware and available, learning from emotion, and navigating difficult emotions.

Being Emotionally Aware and Available

The 13th Century poet and mystic Rumi suggests that being human is like being "a guest house," with all kinds of emotions showing up at the door—and advises us to invite in whatever guest show up, however threatening they may seem, because we never know what gifts they may have for us.

To be available to your emotions means that when they come knocking—however distracting or uncomfortable they may appear—welcome them in. Invite, embrace, and honor the full range of feeling, both pleasurable and disturbing, that you encounter in yourself and others—in the name of expanding your heart's capacity to engage deeply with the adventure of life.

PARADIGM SHIFT ALERT
From: If you can't feel something nice, don't feel anything at all.
To: Feel everything. It makes you more present and available for the richness of life and connection to others.

My wife is one of my greatest teachers in the arena of emotional availability. She cries easily. Occasionally out of sadness, but mostly out of joy, or because she is deeply moved by something she hears or sees or feels that resonates deeply inside her. When she was in her twenties working in the advertising industry in London, she once cried while viewing an ad her agency was working on. Her boss shamed her for letting her emotion show—ironically in a business that is all about eliciting emotion. Unfortunately, my wife's story is not unusual. The world over, to varying degrees, our emotions are undervalued at best, and shamed at worst—often most harshly by ourselves.

Oftentimes we reject our emotions because we're afraid of what might happen if we express them. So we deny what we're feeling. What's important to see is that denying emotion is different from composure. Avoiding what we feel is a reaction to our discomfort, while composure is a choice we make regarding expression and impact. Being aware and available to your feelings does not mean you have to allow yourself to get carried away on their currents. It means giving yourself the choice of if, how, and when you want to express what you feel.

And it isn't just the *negative* emotions, like anger, sadness, and fear—that we tend to avoid or stuff. Some people also have difficulty connecting with *positive* feelings of joy, delight, excitement, or ecstasy—afraid of appearing silly or not being taken seriously.

Research psychologist Brené Brown, in her TED™ talk *The Power of Vulnerability*, says, "You can't selectively numb emotion." When you numb yourself to negative emotion, you become less available to the many flavors of joy. Both negative and positive, your feelings are an essential part of what it means to be human. When you judge any of your emotions as wrong or bad or embarrassing, and push them away, stuff them, or cut yourself off from them, you cut yourself off from your humanity and what makes life rich, and you disconnect from much of your creative energy.

The more that you can be available to your emotions—both positive and negative—the more power they have to *move you*, meaning deepening your connection to yourself and your world, as well as motivating you to take action. Marketeers have made billions on the back of this truth—that we are moved by emotion to buy things, make big decisions, and even change our lives.

In my own experience, when I have allowed myself to feel deep sadness or regret about the impact of some habitual behavior that is getting in my way or hurting others, my pain has been an intense motivator for change. In the same vein, I have learned that being angry with myself can be a potent force propelling me out of complacency. At other times, it's my excitement or joy that pulls me toward something different.

Listening to Emotion

In addition to letting your emotions connect you to the adventure of life, let them give you information about what's going on in your life, and the world around you. While many people, especially in the professional arena, see emotion as mostly something to either avoid or keep in close check, it's more empowering to hold feelings as having something to teach you. Rather than hoping that feelings will bug off so you can get down to business again, get curious—ask yourself what the emotion in the space might suggest. Instead of telling yourself you shouldn't be feeling anger or sadness or too much excitement, ask yourself what your emotion is telling *you*.

When you're aware of emotion—whether yours or others'—you have access to the undercurrents of what's going on in a conversation, a meeting, or your own internal thought processes. Emotional awareness is like an attuned ear. By learning to listen to emotion, rather than ignoring it or reacting to it, you gain insight into information under the surface of things.

PARADIGM SHIFT ALERT
From: Emotions at work are embarrassing at worst, and irrelevant at best.
To: Emotions at work are an important source of information about what is happening in interactions, relationships, team dynamics, and decision-making processes.

For example, if you're frustrated in a meeting, instead of writing off the meeting as a waste of time or saying something you wish you hadn't, get curious about your frustration. It may be a hint that there's an idea or insight that hasn't yet come to the surface, or that there's an important aspect of the meeting process that's being skipped over. Your frustration may be a sign that you need to tune in with more rigor, rather than check out or blow up. The same thing could be said of boredom. If you're bored in a conversation, ask yourself why. What's the real issue that's not being surfaced? What are you doing or thinking that's keeping you from being fully engaged?

When you start appreciating emotion as something to learn from, you'll look for more exact language to describe it—because the particular kind of emotion you are feeling will indicate what to get curious about. Most people have a hard time being specific about what they're feeling, limiting their emotional vocabulary to "great," "ok," or "lousy." The more specifically you can identify what you feel, or what someone else feels, the more adept you will become at listening to emotion to flag what's going on.

A place to start in identifying feelings is to recognize four basic currents—joy, anger, sadness, and fear. Most emotions are some flavor of these four. Flavors of anger for example are frustration, resentment, rage, annoyance. Sadness may show up as grief or melancholy. Fear can look like anxiety, nervousness, or terror. And flavors of joy include feelings like delight and excitement.

Because emotion mostly runs under the surface of things as undercurrent, it takes a strong intention to actually stop and pay attention to the movement of feelings under the surface. Therefore, a key to listening to emotion is cultivating the stillness required to become aware of what you or others are feeling, and thus access the information available.

Stillness also enables your emotions to catch up with your mental speed and the impulse to react without fully thinking something through. There are too many emails fired off, or rants indulged in, that don't wait for emotions to have a chance to settle out into useful information instead of ammunition. When you take a moment to be still, you can tune in and let your emotions inform your thoughts, giving you a chance to craft more strategic and care-full responses.

Navigating Discomfort and Upset

As you move deeper into what it means to lean in, you encounter the challenge of keeping your heart open in the face of pain—your own or another's. You're challenged to be available to not only what feels good, but what's uncomfortable or upsetting to feel. To actually lean into challenging feelings, especially painful ones, is a mark of courage.

It's particularly courageous to stay openhearted in the face of a perceived offense—someone's blame, criticism, or anger directed at you. It takes both awareness and courage to not get defensive. An effective practice in this moment is to simply breathe. Tell yourself that what's going on is not as personal as it seems. The anger or disappointment coming at you may be as much or more about the other person, their perceptions and relationship with themselves, as it is about you.

A client of mine had a boss who would at times lose her cool and blame him for all the troubles of the business, deeply offending his sense of honor, his value for fairness, and his belief in his own integrity. His challenge was to stay engaged in the work, and in the relationship, in the face of what felt offensive. As he leaned in to that challenge, he began to realize that his biggest enemy was his own anger—which he came to realize could inform and motivate him, or it could derail him. It was his choice—and he chose to experience his anger as a reminder of his core values, and motivate him to take a stand for those values. He chose to see his anger as an indicator of how deeply he cared about the business, rather than to let it destroy the relationship and keep him from making the difference he was there to make.

Not only is it important to keep your heart open when someone offends or disappoints you, but also when you let yourself down. When that happens, instead of beating yourself up, practice self-compassion—which doesn't mean self-indulgence, but rather self-care. When you get down on yourself for letting yourself down, you burn the painful experience deeper into your psyche. When you forgive yourself and commit to learning, you make room for a new, more creative behavior.

Perhaps the most intense challenge of navigating difficult emotion is in the face of someone else's pain that you are contributing to. In my own experience of ending a marriage, I found my partner's pain excruciating. I had to learn to acknowledge the hurt she was experiencing without seeing myself as a villain, and without making her wrong or bad in order to make myself feel better about leaving the marriage.

When you lean into your own or others feelings of pain, anger, or sadness—which means not dismissing them with a sarcastic comment, a fake smile, or a false imperviousness—you are staying real. With that authenticity also comes responsibility for your own emotion, experiencing it without blaming someone else for it. By staying both real and responsible, you're inviting the same in others. This can lead to creative conversations that you might not otherwise have, breakthroughs in relationship, or opportunities to set compassionate but firm boundaries.

PARADIGM SHIFT ALERT
From: Difficult emotion is to be avoided or made to go away as quickly as possible.
To: Difficult emotion is to be honored and listened to for the information and cleansing it can bring, then let go of as its service to your emotional presence is completed.

Take anger for instance. Some people have little control over their expression of anger. Others have too much control. In general, a good rule of thumb is that it can be generative to share your anger with people, but rarely is it helpful to point it at them. While spewing your anger at people is almost always reactive, so is stuffing it. Anger needs an outlet—so find ways to let it out where it won't do damage. Try venting with a neutral party who is willing to listen, or cursing under your breath in private, or writing an angry letter that you immediately throw away. Own your feelings as your own, connected to an event or an interaction, but not caused by it. This is an important aspect of what it means to be radically responsible.

When it comes to negative emotion, aside from stuffing or spewing, some people are addicted. It's not uncommon for someone to be addicted to sadness, or even misery. I've known people who seem to be addicted to being annoyed. It's as if there is some sort of pay-off to experiencing the negative emotion. This type of reactivity can go on undetected, and unaddressed, unless we tune in to our emotions and ask ourselves whether they are authentic responses to what's occurring in our lives, or they are unexamined emotional crutches.

- What are my emotions telling me in this moment?
- (When feeling unfairly blamed, criticized or judged) What does it look like to keep my heart open in this moment? Why should I?

Braving Connection

I recall a powerful moment with a client—the CEO of a globally respected talent agency. On the first day of his 3-day Executive Wisdom Quest, we were debriefing feedback from his team and employees, and started to talk about the discipline of courage, the practice of vulnerability, and the power of the heart to create authentic human connection. There was a pause, and a tear rolled down his cheek for the first time in many years. Softly he said, "I must be a nightmare to work for."

This was *not* a moment of weakness. It was a moment of courage. This tough, supremely self-assured, and successful CEO's heart had opened, wide enough to recognize the reality of his impact, and embrace it. We had created an environment where he could be vulnerable, letting down his guard and seeing the gap between who he wanted to be and how he was actually showing up, and feeling the pain of that gap directly without self-judgment or a need to protect or defend.

In that moment, my CEO friend/client opened his heart to— meaning connected with—his own feelings as well as the experience of others.

Seeing and Being Seen

The two most essential elements of connection are empathy and vulnerability—in other words, seeing and feeling others, and allowing yourself to be seen and felt. In the movie Avatar, the native people of the planet Pandora expressed their respect for and connection to one another through the words "I see you."

Seeing and being seen is a way of describing what it means to be in intimate connection. If you have thought of intimacy up until now as a euphemism for sexuality, consider an expanded definition. A way of thinking about Intimacy is *in-to-me-you-see*. It is being willing and available to see and be seen—to allow someone into your inner world, and to feel into the experience of another.

In *Daring Greatly*, Brené Brown says courage means "to tell your story with your whole heart." This means being willing to share what it's like to be you. It means being willing to be seen in all your brilliance as well as in your failures and imperfections.

Being willing to be seen begins with self-acceptance and being basically comfortable with who you are. If you're hiding things from yourself, or hanging on to shame about some aspects of who you are, you're likely to hide those aspects from others. So the journey of knowing and accepting yourself is the place to start.

When you are willing to be seen for all of who you are, you share your struggles. You admit when you don't know, or are out of your depth. While there is a risk of judgment, criticism, or lost opportunity in that level of self-disclosure, the potential upside is trust, admiration and opportunity for connection.

Being seen means you fake it less, and stop trying to impress and look good. Being self-sufficient, accomplished, and competent is not something anyone can be all of the time, so rather than expecting that of yourself, ask for help. Then, actually let people help you—it builds collaboration, and often leads to better ideas. Take yourself off the pedestal. Be honest about what you can do, and what you can't—it makes you more credible and available to connection.

Allowing yourself to be seen helps others understand what makes you tick. It creates understanding of motivations, intentions, insecurities and personality quirks. It makes you more authentic to others and can head off a great deal of miscommunication and misunderstanding.

While your willingness to be seen is primarily an exercise in overriding your discomfort with others seeing your struggles or doubts, it can also be a bit uncomfortable to share your triumphs, joys, and confidence. You might feel that sharing your success may evoke envy. If that's the case, rather than hide your brilliance, share it with sensitivity to impact, but also without apology.

PARADIGM SHIFT ALERT
From: Vulnerability—allowing your struggles, fears, and doubts to be seen by others—is weakness.
To: Vulnerability is strength. It takes courage and an ability to be in open-hearted relationship with the feelings that come with being exposed, instead of in reaction to those feelings.

While being seen empowers your relationships, not every situation calls for full visibility. There are times when being seen for all of who you are can be emotionally or professionally dangerous. The practice is to push the edges of your comfort zone and stretch how much you are willing to be seen, while at the same time being smart about it.

Being smart about it also means not mistaking a visible heart with wearing it on your sleeve—which tends toward drama, distraction, and manipulation—through ranting, going overboard with tears, pouting, etc.. The point is to be real while also paying attention to the impact of your authenticity. Be judicious about how much you express your emotions, and be intentional about what that expression is serving. Is your intention to get attention and create drama, or to foster greater openness, candidness, and trust?

The intimacy created by allowing yourself to be seen is complemented by being willing and able to see others and feel into their experience. This is the practice of empathy.

An underlying mindset essential to empathy is valuing others for who they are beyond the roles they play in your life—whether it's boss, spouse, parent, or janitor—and specifically valuing their emotional experience. This is done by practicing three key elements of empathy—witnessing, validating, and resisting the urge to fix.

To witness another's feelings is to respond to the emotion you see in a way that communicates to the other person you have seen him or her. Naming the feeling, for example. Or a hand on their shoulder. Or an exclamation of excitement for them.

To validate emotion is to refrain from judging it as right or wrong, or justified or not justified. It's critical to understand that witnessing and validating emotion is not about judging it as good or bad. You honor someone's right to feel what they're feeling, independent from your thoughts about it. This is especially difficult—and especially important—when you find yourself feeling blamed as the cause of someone's hurt. In that case, it's especially important to not tell them what they should or shouldn't feel. If you can, expand your heart enough to let their emotions be what they are, as crazy or unjustified as those feelings may seem to you.

Lastly, it's important to refrain from fixing difficult emotions. Resist saying, "It's okay," to dismiss emotion because often, it just isn't. And don't fix it. Don't offer solutions to get the person out of their pain as quickly as possible, which can leave them feeling unseen. When someone is really in the throes of intense emotion, they are usually not available for creative problem solving.

PARADIGM SHIFT ALERT
From: Intimacy is reserved for lovers in the bedroom.
To: Intimacy is seeing and being seen—being both empathetic and vulnerable—which builds trust and credibility in all your relationships.

Choosing Trust

Being willing to be vulnerable and empathetic is fundamentally a choice to trust. It's not trusting that you'll never be let down or hurt. And it's not trusting a particular person because they have proven themselves trustworthy. It's trusting yourself to be responsible (response-able) in relationship. This means trusting yourself to set appropriate boundaries, make clear agreements, not shy away from tension and conflict, and give your energy to relationships in a way that doesn't deplete you. This is vulnerable because choosing trust is letting go of controlling anything other than your own thoughts, emotions, and behavior.

Putting your focus on choosing to trust yourself first is a fundamental departure from the conventional view of trust, which focuses entirely on trusting others. Most of us have learned to trust others when they act the way we expect them to, when they share our values, and when they keep their promises. We stop trusting others when they let us down in some way, or when we judge them as unworthy of our trust.

The radical shift in paradigm is from trusting others based on our judgments of them, to choosing to trust others based on our willingness to trust ourselves and to build trust in relationship.

When you trust your own ability to create safety in relationship, your experience of trust with others becomes simple, and is comprised of three things. First you trust that another person is doing the best they can at any given time with the level of awareness and capability they have. Second, you take responsibility for assessing whether you want to rely on them in a particular situation, or for a particular deliverable—whether that's faithfulness as a spouse, or willingness and ability to execute as a business partner or direct report. And third, you take responsibility for the quality of communication and connection that creates the reliability you need in the relationship.

PARADIGM SHIFT ALERT

From: Trust is something we extend to people when they don't let us down, or when we judge them as trustworthy because they have similar values or perspectives.

To: Trust is something we choose to build with people because we have confidence in our ability to be response-able and co-creative in relationship.

Notice that this way of thinking, while radical, is extremely empowering. It takes your experience of trust out of the hands of others, and puts it in your own hands. While there will always be times when others break agreements with you, your experience of trust becomes dependent not on what they do, but on what you choose to do in response. You empower yourself to assess, based on the magnitude of the trespass or the frequency of it, whether you want to continue making agreements with that person and relying on them to deliver. It's important to distinguish assessment from judgment. In assessment, you are asking yourself, "Given my experience of the other person, how do I choose to engage?" This is a different question from, "Is this person trustworthy?" And while it may seem like a subtle distinction, it has huge consequences. When you focus on how you choose to relate to someone, rather than on your judgment of them, then you stop trying to control the behavior of others to make them trustworthy in your eyes. Instead, you put your focus on yourself—on communicating and relating in a way that creates the experience of trust.

Ultimately, this is what it means to trust—to let go of trying to control others' behavior and focus on choosing your own thoughts, feelings, and actions. It's vulnerable and courageous because there's nowhere to look for trust but inside yourself. The exciting part is that choosing to trust sends a signal to others and to your own subconscious mind that your experience of life does not depend on how others behave. In a paradoxical way, the vulnerability of your willingness to trust becomes your strength.

Letting Go

So far, in exploring the practice of braving connection, we've focused on the kind of heart-strength, or courage, it takes to create authentic intimate connection—namely vulnerability and empathy, and choosing to trust.

A third element is letting go. It may be the bravest aspect of connection because one's willingness to let go of what feels safe is what most enables a truly full-on sense of connection—whether that's with another person or with the journey of life itself.

I'm sure I was in my teens when I first saw the quote, "A ship in a harbor is safe, but that's not what ships are built for." Hearts are built for connection, and connection isn't always safe. Hearts are built for adventuring out into life, and life isn't always safe.

Connection is brave precisely because it is uncertain and impermanent. In other words, paradoxically, connection is strengthened by your willingness to let it go. Being intimate with the important things in your life—health, people, things you love—is a combination of holding onto them dearly, connecting deeply with their preciousness, while at the same time knowing that they will not last forever, and being willing to let them go.

I learned to swim at an early age. I remember the first time I dared to let go of the edge of the swimming pool. The idea of venturing into deep water to doggie-paddle the three feet between me and my dad was terrifying. But I finally did it, beginning a life-long love of swimming. I often think of that moment of letting go of the edge of the pool, and the lesson in it. While letting go made me vulnerable, it also made it possible for me to enlarge my experience of life.

When has letting go opened a door for you to *grow through*, and thereby expand your life? As a leap of faith, letting go sends a message to the Universe that you are ready for something new. And in some quirky, seemingly very unfair way, you often don't get to see what's coming next until you've let go of your current reality and limits, which can feel good because they are comfortable and familiar, even if they're also outworn and painful.

There are times when *being willing to let go* is actually what it takes to *keep something* that you are meant to hold onto. Sometimes all that's really necessary for something new to occur is a *willingness* to let go. Being willing to let go of something—be it a job, a client, a marriage, or an outgrown way of relating to a child—can be enough to change the nature of your relationship with that thing. When you take the energy of clinging to something out of the equation, you change the equation. You may end up staying in the job or the marriage, but in a new way. In other words, you may not end up letting go of the actual thing or situation itself, but let go of a way of being or a way of relating. By letting go of an old mindset or behavior, you create an opening for change to occur.

Because change, and the letting go that it requires, can feel painful, you may be tempted to keep some emotional distance from aspects of life you almost certainly will need to let go of at some point. Some people make the mistake of never really getting attached to anything to avoid the pain of letting go. From one perspective, this makes sense. Who wants pain? But from another perspective, the joy, love, connection, and intimacy we lose by never really attaching can be greater than the inevitable loss that comes with the eventual letting go. There is a beautiful and powerful paradox available here that will keep you in the place of being achingly wholehearted. The paradox is letting yourself get close to things in life, while also being willing to let them go when the time comes.

PARADIGM SHIFT ALERT
From: The willingness to let go means you're not committed to the connection.
To: The willingness to let go is essential to experiencing deep connection because it means you've stopped protecting and withholding your heart.

Embracing this paradox is the key to real connection. In any genuine connection, there is the potential for loss. Letting go means being willing to experience that loss—whether it's of our own choosing or not. The ending of a marriage could be something we choose, or not. Similarly, with the loss of a job. A loved one's death is a loss we have nothing to say about. Either way—whether you choose the loss or not—you always have a choice about letting go. We all know someone who has hung on to a loved one too long after they're gone—unwilling to choose the new possibilities that could come with letting go. Or who has stayed in a job because it's safe, even though it may be a dead end, or deadening.

In addition to being willing to embrace the experience of loss, we must also embrace our fear of loss—the fear that inevitably arises with contemplating our dreams, and realizing there will be things we need to leave behind as we go in search of them. And the fear of failing to get what we're reaching for when we let go of what we have. When you can arrive at some inner peace in relation to your fear of both losing what you're leaving behind, and not getting what you're going for, then you can actually do the letting go that is necessary to move toward your dreams and visions.

Shortly after turning 80, my mother was thrown from her horse and suffered a concussion. She had been riding horses her entire life. Her days in Colorado and Arizona were centered around riding in the wilderness and caring for her horses. We all knew there would come a day when she would have to let go of her beloved way of life. That it would become too dangerous and strenuous for her aging body, even though it fed her spirit so deeply. When that day finally came, when she knew she could not take the chance of another fall, my mother gracefully let go. She found new owners for her horses, sold her trailer and truck, and grieved her loss. She could have slid into depression or inactivity. Instead, she chose to look for something new and fulfilling to give her life energy to— workshops to attend, volunteering, short walks in beautiful places. Her willingness to let go, including reaching out to something new, was vulnerable, courageous, and ultimately empowering.

The ultimate in letting go is connected to the ultimate in holding on—to life itself. There comes a time for each of us when we have to let go of life. Letting go of things, experiences, ways of being, and people while we're alive is practice for that eventual *great letting go*. It is never a question of *if*, but always a question of *with what grace*. The times of letting go of things, relationships, places and circumstances in your life are actually opportunities to practice the grace needed for that ultimate letting go.

ACTIVATION QUESTIONS
- What does it look like in this moment, in this relationship, to be authentically vulnerable or empathetic?
- What in this moment do I need to let go of? Why?

Living in Appreciation

Appreciation is a powerful force. To live in appreciation is to expand your positive connection to the world around you, and your potency in it. To withhold or stifle appreciation, on the other hand, limits the flow of connection, understanding, abundance, power, and love.

Being a Person of Increase

When you appreciate, you become what early 20th Century author Wallace Wattles coined "a person of increase." Meaning that what you appreciate, actually appreciates. In other words, your appreciation has an amplifying effect. It is absolutely an investment, guaranteed to get a positive return. Appreciation shines a light on the positive stuff going on. When you dig deep for appreciation, going beyond the run-of-the-mill obvious things to appreciate to the less obvious, you ferret out hidden beauty and genius.

At work, to give appreciation is one of the most powerful leadership practices. Without it, attention to excellence stagnates or shrinks. When people contribute—even when they're paid for it—and are not appreciated, their motivation to contribute tapers off. Unless highly motivated from within, they slip into a *why bother* attitude. They stop going the extra mile, and start contributing just enough to keep their jobs. They may keep performing, but only as long as they have nowhere better to go.

All people—and not just your work colleagues by the way, but also your spouse and kids—naturally want to stretch and grow in their capabilities. But at the same time we are tempted to succumb to the gravity of our comfort zones. Appreciation can make the difference between going for the stretch, and staying comfortable.

We all want and need to be seen. To feel unacknowledged is a powerful *de*-motivator. Just check in with your own experience for the truth of that. This doesn't mean everyone wants to be in the limelight, or get public accolades. But we all want our value to be recognized in some way. Acknowledgment can be as simple as noticing the high quality of someone's work, and commenting on it. The more specific you can be, the better. Instead of "Hey, great design," it would be more specific and impactful if you said something like, "I really like the simplicity and boldness of that design."

Appreciate people not only for the contributions they make, but for who they are. Praising someone for who they are may take more thoughtfulness on your part, but it can be extremely powerful. For example, you might say to someone, "I see you as incredibly courageous." Or, "You were such a calming presence in the room." Or, "Your directness and honesty inspire me."

PARADIGM SHIFT ALERT
From: Appreciation is a waste of time, or worse—it's coddling.
To: Appreciation is an essential enabler of engagement, motivation, belonging, resilience, and innovation—not just in professional life, but personal and family life as well.

The power of appreciation becomes most apparent when looking at its opposite. Have you ever felt devalued in a meeting, or one-on-one conversation? Have you experienced your ideas being dismissed? The eye rolling that is way too common in team meetings and dinner-table conversations is also way more harmful than most people realize.

The opportunity to appreciate someone often becomes painfully apparent to me when I fail to take advantage of it. Sales clerks come to mind. Or call center associates. There's the occasional rudeness that makes me a jerk. But there's also the less obvious missed opportunity to say a few kind words of praise. I regret those missed opportunities because the world is so hungry for appreciation.

In the business world, many leaders still hold the mindset that people shouldn't need to be appreciated beyond their paycheck, thinking, "We're all grown-ups here, just do your job." That way of thinking may be a smokescreen for, "I don't know how to appreciate people, and it makes me feel uncomfortable." It's good to stretch your appreciation muscle for the sake of building both relationships and results.

Appreciation builds healthier culture, whether it's in your family or your business—one where people feel a sense of belonging, and therefore engagement and commitment. If you're interested in talent retention (or spousal retention!), there is no better investment than appreciation. People tend to be more committed to places and situations to which they feel they belong.

In addition to praise for the people around you, it is extremely important, and often more difficult, to extend the same to yourself. Self-appreciation helps you become more resourced. And it helps you stretch and grow, because when you're feeling good about yourself, you're more available to openly look at mistakes or shortcomings and learn from them.

Appreciating the Hard Stuff

Life does not always present a face you want to appreciate. All too often, what we see—both in the world around us, and in our inner world—evokes more disgust than immediate appreciation. Or what we see evokes pain, anger, frustration, and grief. These are the times when it's hardest to practice appreciation, yet also most empowering and transformative.

Consider appreciating the most difficult events and circumstances in life as opportunities to hone your ability to creatively respond with what's best in you. This goes a long way in dissipating any resistance you have to what life brings. As the saying goes, "What you resist persists." What you don't resist becomes something that can be potentially transformed, or at the least it can be an opportunity to show up with grace.

Nelson Mandela is an extreme, and yet very real example of the power of appreciation amidst the most difficult circumstances of life. He used much of his 28 years in prison to build his capability to be an incredible force for positive change in his world. Instead of wallowing in misery and resentment, which are forms of resistance to one's circumstances, he chose to use his time in captivity to promote freedom.

It's a rare person who hasn't been dealt difficult or traumatic cards in life. Cancer, car accidents, betrayals, corporate downsizing—the list goes on. How we play the hand we're dealt says a lot about our Courage. Not in the sense of toughing it out, but in the sense of keeping our hearts open—versus turning bitter and cynical. My good friend Jim Anderson, author of *Behind Every Dark Cloud is a Silver Lining*, when faced with upsets in life asks, "Why is this perfect for me now?" His provocative question is the epitome of this mindset of appreciation for whatever life brings, especially when it's tough.

It's important that you don't confuse appreciating the hard

stuff with pretending the hard stuff isn't hard. Choosing appreciation doesn't mean you won't feel emotions like anger, frustration, and even revulsion when you encounter difficult circumstances or people in life. What it means is that, alongside those emotions, you find a way to appreciate something in whatever is going on. And as you do, it's likely that your negative emotions will take up less of your attention. They are still there, but you are less controlled by them.

Choosing to appreciate an aspect of a difficult situation or relationship can help a gift to emerge where before you couldn't see anything worthwhile. By getting curious about the learning and growth opportunity that could be there, you actually create that opportunity. You can begin down that path by sending out a simple silent appreciation for the situation and the person. You know you have this opportunity when your thoughts are inclined toward, "I hate it when...," or, "It's driving me crazy that...," or "That f@#*ing @#*^#@...." If you can stop yourself for a moment, and ask how there might be a gift in the situation, you might be amazed at the opportunity for a breakthrough.

Forgiving

When you take appreciating the hard stuff to an even higher level, it brings you to forgiveness. In fact, I like to call forgiveness *radical appreciation* because it is intentionally choosing appreciation over resentment, even in very difficult circumstances.

Most people think of forgiveness as something you do for someone if you're feeling generous enough. But it's really something much larger. Forgiveness is an antioxidant for the soul—your soul. Forgiveness is a heart-healing practice that you choose—over and over—in relation to events, circumstances, and especially other human beings. It is a stand you take in life, rather than something you do in some situations and don't do in others. It's a choice you make, independent of the severity of the transgression. Forgiving is more difficult as the offense or pain gets harder to bear, but when you're practicing forgiveness as a state of being, the situation doesn't dictate whether to practice it or not.

Before we talk more about what practicing forgiveness is, let's say what it's not. Forgiveness does not mean caving in when you should be standing up. Nor is it about excusing bad behavior in another or yourself. Excusing and forgiving are two very different things. To excuse is to fail to be accountable. It is to let someone or yourself off the hook. Genuine forgiveness on the other hand insists on accountability. It includes acknowledging the impact of what has occurred, and doing what is needed to be in the most empowering relationship you can be with the offense and the offender.

The first step in forgiveness is letting go of resentment, which is a catchword for a whole range of angry emotions that can be toxic to your being if left to fester too long. To let go of resentment is not always easy, but definitely empowering and worth the effort.

To let go of resentment, you first have to recognize it. A sure sign that you're holding onto resentment is that you *feel* victimized. And as hard as this might be to acknowledge to yourself, feeling victimized is a choice. Meaning that while you may not have a choice about whether you are a victim of something—someone's action, an illness, an accident—you can choose whether or not to feel victimized. An indication that you've chosen victimization, usually quite unconsciously, is that you're holding onto resentment. You'll notice a desire to blame, punish, hold a grudge, or even get revenge. The pull of that desire might even feel good, oddly enough, touching something in you that takes pleasure in being holier-than-thou or getting back at something or someone outside yourself for the pain you're in.

Next, acknowledge that holding onto resentment is like drinking poison, while expecting it to hurt someone else. Your reactive mind thinks you're punishing the other person. You're not—you're actually punishing yourself with the toxicity you're holding inside.

When you let go of that toxicity, you free up space for appreciation—which begins with considering the possibility of a silver lining, a hidden gift. And, while this next step may seem radical, you can consider embracing a profound paradox that life can be painful and disappointing, while at the same time *perfect*. When you choose to see pain and perfection at the same time—which admittedly is a very tall order—you are opening up possibilities for magic and healing.

PARADIGM SHIFT ALERT
From: Forgiveness is letting someone off the hook.
To: The radical appreciation that is forgiveness is an antioxidant for the soul. It is freeing yourself from the inner toxicity created by holding resentment.

While forgiveness is most often thought of as something you extend to others, the impact of practicing forgiveness with yourself can be equally liberating. If you've ever tried to forgive yourself—and I hope you have, especially for something big—you know it isn't a one-time thing. It's a practice. Over and over, the demons of guilt and shame—which are essentially resentment turned inward—sneak their way into your consciousness, and you choose how to meet them. You take the same elements of forgiveness that liberate you from resentment toward others, and you offer them to yourself—namely, recognizing self-incrimination, seeing its toxicity, and claiming your connection to your best self. You loosen your grip on shame and simultaneously practice self-appreciation.

It's also possible to practice forgiveness in relation to the circumstances of your life. We all know people who seem to feel betrayed by life. They blame life itself for their poor experience of it. That's perhaps extreme, but consider the subtle ways that you might be holding resentment toward things that have happened to you, that you can't blame anyone else for, but nevertheless have felt beyond your control. Things like a loved one dying, a natural disaster, an economic downturn, or a corporate downsizing. These situations are also opportunities for practicing forgiveness as a powerful way to foster growth in yourself, rather than the stagnation that comes from burdening yourself with resentment.

Remember—whether forgiving yourself, life, or another person—it's a practice, and a process. Give yourself permission to start slow and dip your toes in the water. Rather than tackling the situations where you feel deeply offended, betrayed, or wounded, begin with small transgressions and little resentments, and work up from there. Consciously choose to let go of resentment, because the person it hurts most is you. And intentionally choose to appreciate whatever goodness and opportunities you can find in a situation, other people, and yourself.

ACTIVATION QUESTIONS
- (When faced with difficult circumstances) What is the silver lining in this?
- What can I appreciate in myself, another, or the circumstances I'm in? How does that change things?

Defensiveness and Withdrawal
(The Reactive Patterns of Courage)

Defensiveness is Courage distorted. While defensiveness can look like fierce boundaries or courageously standing up for yourself, it is ironically a dead giveaway to the fact that you are not connected to the fiercely open-hearted expansive energy that is actual Courage.

The repression of Courage is withdrawal. Like defensiveness, withdrawal is also a reaction to perceived threat—but a pulling-away reaction rather than a lashing out.

Getting defensive, or withdrawing, are what we do when we react, versus creatively respond, to something we interpret as dangerous. To our reactive selves, defensiveness or withdrawal are perfectly normal and justified ways to meet perceived threat. If we were dogs, defensiveness would look like our hackles going up. Withdrawal would look like tucking our tails. We get defensive or withdraw because we feel under attack in some way, or backed into a corner.

Remember, as you read about defensiveness and withdrawal, that we all are subject to reactivity from time to time through lack of awareness and intention. The inner adventure is to catch ourselves in reaction, and in the spirit of radical responsibility, choose the Discipline over the distortion or repression.

Defensiveness (Courage Distorted)

Reacting to fear and insecurity—When you are defensive, you are contracting your heart. You are closing off to Life, and pushing away whatever makes you uncomfortable, usually as a reaction to some degree of fear. When you are insecure, but can't admit it; when you don't trust yourself, life or others; when your heart is tight or closed—that's the soil in which defensiveness grows.

While defensiveness may look like a kind of confidence because it pushes back, it's actually driven by insecurity. It's an insecurity that we act out aggressively, and in its most extreme forms shows up as being demeaning or bullying. When we show up that way, it's usually because we feel vulnerable, but don't have the awareness to know it, or the courage to admit it. We don't feel worthy enough to be seen and accepted in our own vulnerability, so we push back to protect.

Defensiveness usually shows up when you feel attacked, blamed, or unfairly criticized. When you feel criticized—which can sometimes be more your interpretation of what's being expressed, fueled by your insecurity, than a true assessment of the communication—what you're often defending against is the emotion under the surface that is evoked—like self-doubt, fear of not being enough or of not being accepted, feeling alone or unsupported.

The trigger of shame—Perhaps the most fundamental trigger of defensiveness is shame. Not a feeling of guilt about something we have said or done, but a sense of shame about who we are, or are not. When that sensitive place of shame is awakened by some failure or mistake, or someone's comment, or coming face to face with our negative impact, it's difficult to stay non-defensive.

One of the best ways to recover when your defensiveness kicks in, is not to take things personally. Whatever is happening that is triggering defensiveness is only partially about you. You can choose what to take in, what to take on, and what not to.

Another way to fall into the defensive stance less often is to cultivate a deep and basic sense of worthiness. Tell yourself as often as possible that while you are completely capable of screwing up, you are also completely worthy of connection and a sense of belonging and feeling valued.

When you feel yourself getting defensive, the opportunity is to be aware of the flavor of shame that you may be experiencing in yourself, to stay connected to your courage and keep your heart open, and to appreciate the constructive feedback, or even the grain of truth in the comment, however unfair, false, or mean it seems.

Defensiveness or boundaries—How do you know when you are being defensive, and when you are setting a boundary in a healthy, non-violent way? Notice if you are counter-attacking, or if you are open to looking at yourself, while holding your ground from a place of worthiness and self-authority. Of course, there are times when defensiveness and boundary setting are going on at the same time. The challenge and opportunity is to get better at standing your ground with an open heart.

There are some powerful examples in the world of courage showing up where an aggressively defensive reaction would be, by most conventional thinking, justified. Picture Martin Luther King, and the thousands of people who risked their lives in the non-violent marches and demonstrations of the civil rights movement. Or Gandhi and his non-violent approach to freeing India from British rule. Or the Dalai Lama, offering blessings to the Chinese who occupy his country and oppress its people. If you want to hold an image in mind of what the Discipline of Courage (versus defensiveness) looks like, it would be hard to do better than this.

Withdrawal (Courage Repressed)

On the other end of the spectrum from defensiveness is withdrawal, which occurs for all the same reasons as the more aggressive ways defensiveness shows itself. Withdrawal is just as much a fear-driven, versus courage-driven, reaction as defensiveness is. It is a kind of running away from the perceived threat. If Defensiveness is *fight*, withdrawal is *flight*. It looks like disappearing, hiding, pulling away, running away, or freezing up. It lacks the courage needed to stay in the conversation. The opportunity, when you sense yourself withdrawing, is to stay open, or at least to simply stay present.

You'll notice that you may tend more toward defensiveness, or toward withdrawal—toward fight or toward flight. Which one you fall into may vary depending on who or what your heart is constricting in reaction to, like a spouse or a boss, for example.

ACTIVATION QUESTIONS

- In this moment, is my heart more open, or more closed? More expanded or more contracted?
- (When feeling defensive) What might I be feeling insecure about, or afraid of?

Chapter 5 Summary Points

Courage is loving life—all of it—in a spirit of adventure. It is keeping your heart open and available to life and people, despite the inevitable hurts and setbacks.

Leaning In

Leaning in is embracing emotion as an essential part of life. We are more effective and fulfilled when we value emotion for the information it holds, the juice and intimacy it brings, and the way it connects us to ourselves and others.

Braving Connection

We create intimacy in life, and great relationships at work, through our willingness to be vulnerable—in other words, to be real, exposed, and imperfect—and through our empathy for others. To see and be seen can feel risky, but builds trust and connection.

Braving connection is fundamentally a choice to trust—not that others will always deliver, but that you will always be able to take care of yourself in relationship.

The most intimate kind of connection is enabled by your willingness to let go—to let go of pretense, of being unassailable, and eventually of life itself.

Living in Appreciation

What you appreciate, appreciates. Seeing the value in others and acknowledging it creates upward spirals of excellence, belonging, commitment, and confidence.

To appreciate the hard stuff, and to practice the *radical appreciation* that is forgiveness, creates opportunities for growth and healing.

Defensiveness and Withdrawal

Defensiveness is the distortion of Courage, arising from a sense of insecurity and feeling of being under threat. Defensiveness is reacting to perceived attack by closing down your heart. Withdrawal is a repression of Courage, also a reaction to fear. One is fight, while the other is flight. They are equally harmful to your relationships and experience of life.

Chapter 5 Journaling

The emotions that are most uncomfortable for me to lean into are...
Because...

What it would take for me to be even more courageous and wholehearted, versus anxious, in my life and relationships is...

Aspects of myself that I tend to hide from others are things like...

What appreciation does for me in my life is...

The situations in which I get defensive or withdraw are...
The impact is...
What I could do to stay more open hearted is...

Warm-up Questions

- How aware am I of the assumptions I make, and beliefs I hold, about myself, others, circumstances, and the world?

- How good am I at listening to and valuing others' points of view when I have a strong perspective of my own?

- How consciously and intentionally do I envision the experience of life and work I want to have?

- To what degree am I critical and judgmental? And when I am, why?

Clarity

CLARITY IS the discipline of meeting yourself and others in a space of open-minded engagement. Rather than being certain about what you know, or insisting that you're right about it, Clarity is being curious while also being willing to express a thoughtful point of view.

Clarity elevates the quality of your conversation—first with yourself in your own head, and then in the way you listen and communicate with others—and thus refines the quality of your experience in life and presence with yourself and others.

What Clarity is: being curious while discerning
What Clarity does: elevates the conversation
Distortion: judgment
Repression: confusion

PARADIGM SHIFT ALERT
From: Clarity is something that you arrive at, ending the conversation.
To: Clarity is a discipline that you practice, elevating the conversation.

Practicing the discipline of Clarity means being curious, open, discerning, and intentional with your thoughts and communication. It means the contents of your mind look more like awareness and wisdom, and less like chatter, harsh judgment, or confusion. My father used to say to me, more often than I like to admit, "Burke, use your head." Clarity is using your head in a way that empowers.

Clarity Archetypes: Sage and Educator

The Sage embodies the wisdom of the intellect. It is the one in you who thinks deeply, incisively, and critically, without being judgmental of other people and points of view. This is the one who assesses, strategizes, and discerns. Your sage is aware of your beliefs and chooses ones that empower you and others.

The Educator in you is the one who is curious about the world. It is the part of you that seeks out knowledge and understanding, and shares insights and experience with others, without being didactic. Your educator is a master at asking great questions to draw out wisdom in others.

Recall that archetypes are universally recognized energetic signatures. They represent a whole constellation of attitudes, skills, and ways of being with a particular genius to them.

Take a moment now to visualize and feel the Sage and the Educator in you—and the degrees to which you are familiar with them and have access to their particular energies.

The Core Practices of Clarity

Holding Empowering Narratives

Uncovering beliefs that limit you, and authoring stories that empower you.

Valuing Diverse Perspectives

Valuing diverse views, while also having a strong point of view of your own.

Expanding Your Vision

Perceiving the past, present, and future in ways that empower you and others to create a more generative and fulfilling experience of life.

The Practice Elements

Holding Empowering Narratives

» Listening to your stories

» Seeing limiting beliefs

» Choosing empowering narratives

Valuing Diverse Perspectives

» Letting go of having the one right answer

» Drawing out diverse perspectives

» Creating from competing points of view

Expanding Your Vision

» Learning from the past

» Focusing on present opportunity

» Imagining what can be

The Reactive Patterns of Clarity

Judgment

Confusion

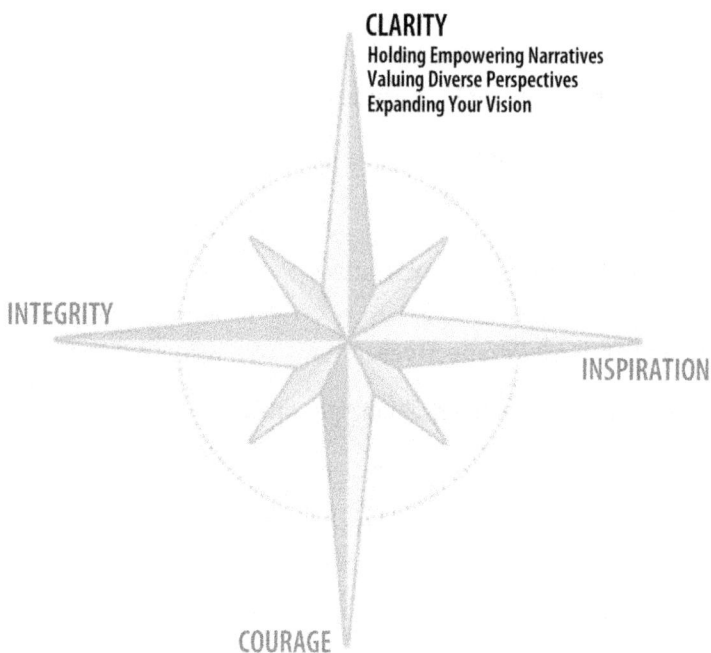

CLARITY
Holding Empowering Narratives
Valuing Diverse Perspectives
Expanding Your Vision

INTEGRITY

INSPIRATION

COURAGE

Holding Empowering Narratives

Whether aware of it or not, you tell yourself stories. You are engaged in an ongoing narrative that has a wide array of storylines covering just about everything—from specific situations, other people, and the world around you, to your capabilities, your preferences, and your own body. The stories you tell yourself are almost entirely unconscious, unless you intentionally bring them into conscious awareness. To make your unconscious narratives conscious is an example of engaging with leadership as sacred work, and taking radical responsibility seriously.

The thing about your stories is—they're always creating something. Sometimes what they create is liberating and empowering, and other times not. It bears repeating—*your narratives are always creating something!* The question is, "What kind of experience and impact are you creating with the narratives you hold?" And the practice is becoming aware of your stories and what they are creating in your life; and then choosing them more intentionally.

Listening to Your Stories

Becoming aware of your stories is a process of learning to listen to your thoughts. This is a powerful and appropriate use of your mind—to observe your own thoughts and the impact they're having on you and how you show up in your world.

As you observe your thoughts and the stories you tell yourself, resist writing them off as *just stories*, but rather recognize that they carry significant weight in your own mind. Your narratives are what you believe is true—in other words, they are your beliefs—and sometimes tightly-held beliefs. For example, people used to believe the earth was flat. Now, we believe things like "You have to be charismatic to be a great leader"; "The more hours you work, the more dedicated you are"; "It's not professional to show emotion at work"; "Men are..."; "Women are...." The list goes on.

Some of your stories are about you. Some are about your world. Your stories about the world often come in the form of biases—beliefs you hold about types of people or the lifestyles they choose. It is an essential act of consciousness and generosity to admit that you have biases—whether they are racial, gender-based, ethnocentric, or other.

Biases are cousin to assumptions, which are unexamined stories. By becoming aware of your assumptions and being transparent about them, you create opportunities for potentially transformative conversation. Being transparent with your assumptions can sound something like "I realize I've been assuming that..., and I want to check it out with you." When you have a conversation, or read an email, ask yourself what assumptions you are making about another person, their communication, and their motivations. You may be surprised by what you've been assuming. More importantly, you can use your assumption-awareness to engage with people differently. For example, you may have been assuming that someone's curt email style means they're unfriendly or they don't like you, which might cause you to distance yourself. Instead, you could choose to stay open and curious, letting your own best intentions, rather than your assumptions about them, drive how you engage or communicate.

I sometimes play a game with myself when I'm driving, or sitting in a coffee shop or in a meeting. I'll challenge myself to notice the assumptions and biases—which are actually forms of judgment—that I have about the people I come across. It's amazing to see how subtle and yet pervasive my judgments are. What's even more interesting to me is recognizing that my biases and assumptions actually say more about me than about the people they're directed at. For example, when I see someone who is physically out of shape, I can assume they're lazy. My judgment about them reflects the way I am hard on myself about my level of fitness, and harsh in what I think it means about me.

PARADIGM SHIFT ALERT
From: One should never make assumptions.
To: While it's true that assuming can make "an ass out of you and me (ass-u-me)," it is almost impossible to avoid making assumptions. The point is to be aware of yourself making an assumption, reflect on what it reveals about you and how you think, be transparent about it when appropriate, and check it out to see if it's actually true.

As you get better at listening to your biases, assumptions, and stories, you start to see that they tend to operate as self-fulfilling prophecy. The tighter you hold them, the more you have experiences that reinforce them. They become truer in your own mind and more real in your experience.

If you say repeatedly to yourself, "work is crazy," you are likely to experience more craziness. If you operate from the belief that you're the smartest person in the room, you may keep finding that you experience no one's ideas as being as good as yours. But if you believe everyone has an important contribution to make, you may find yourself surrounded by really smart people—not because all of a sudden they got smarter, but because your belief about you and them has changed.

In addition to feeding self-fulfilling prophecy, beliefs drive behavior. If you believe that life is hard, shit happens, and people are only out for themselves, you'll behave differently and experience life differently than if you think instead that magic happens or people are fundamentally compassionate and generous. If you believe someone doesn't deserve a seat at the table, you'll probably ignore their perspective. If you believe someone is flakey, or too rigid, or too political, you'll be less open to their ideas. If you believe someone is brilliant, you'll listen carefully. And if you believe they're well intentioned, you'll hear good intentions behind their words.

The most obvious way that disempowering beliefs about yourself drive ineffective behavior is through acting out the belief. Another way is through trying to disprove the belief you're holding. This often results in over-compensating behavior. For example, if your belief is that you're not as smart as you should be for the job you're in, you may keep trying to prove that you really do deserve your position. This can create an impression of low confidence. It can also detract from the quality of your contribution because your focus on proving yourself causes you to be more concerned about others' perceptions of you than the ways you are contributing. Your efforts to disprove your disempowering belief, and prove yourself, often end up backfiring.

Seeing Limiting Beliefs

As you become more adept at listening to your stories, you will see that some narratives empower you, and others limit you. It's important to pay attention to both.

If you think about it, you will notice that many of the behaviors you feel good about, or that are effective, are driven by empowering beliefs. Perhaps you see yourself as a strong person. Or you believe that you are capable of achieving whatever goals you set for yourself. You are likely to take positive and effective action toward those goals.

On the other hand, we all carry beliefs around with us that are limiting. When your limiting beliefs run contrary to your espoused values and highest aspirations, this creates inner conflict and confusion, which then impacts your behavior. For example, you might hold courageous authenticity as a core value, but at the same time have an unconscious limiting belief that says, "What I think or feel isn't that important." So you don't speak up because your limiting belief overrides your value for courageous authenticity. Or you might value trust, but have a core limiting belief that people will take advantage of you if you're not hyper vigilant, which leads you to keep your distance and keep your cards close to your chest.

Some of your limiting beliefs are about you—about who you believe you are (not enough, not loveable, etc.), what you believe you are capable of (not able to, not good at, etc.), and what you believe you are worthy of (don't deserve, not worthy of, etc.). Other limiting beliefs are about other people or the world and life in general. For example, "Life is not fair." Or, "Most people can't be trusted."

Beliefs that you have not consciously chosen are your *default* or *conditioned* beliefs. Many of these originated through your family and culture as beliefs that you have unconsciously accepted as your own. Your default beliefs also come from interpreting your experience. When you experience something, you automatically—and usually subconsciously—interpret that experience, and then turn your interpretation into a belief, which often reinforces an already-held default belief. As the bumper-sticker-worthy mantra goes, "Don't believe everything you think." In other words, your interpretive thinking isn't always worthy of becoming a belief.

When you see where a belief comes from, you can understand that it might have been true at one time, but is no longer true, or that it is someone else's story that you have adopted, and isn't actually true for you. Either way, your insight into the origin of the belief helps you to see it for what it is, and enables you to loosen its hold on you.

For example, let's say you had a repeated experience in childhood of being one of the last picked when you and your friends were choosing sides for the soccer game on the playground. You interpreted that experience to mean that you were non-athletic, and carry this belief into adulthood, even as your body becomes more coordinated and capable. The belief, which is no longer actually true, may still hold you back. Because you are still carrying the belief that you are non-athletic, you may pass up the pleasure of playing beach volleyball with friends or kicking the soccer ball around with your kids. When you can see how your belief is operating, and how it is limiting you, you are more able to drop it in favor of a new belief.

PARADIGM SHIFT ALERT
From: Most of what limits you is from the external world—people, events, and circumstances in your life.
To: What limits you most is your inner world—the thoughts, assumptions, and beliefs you hold about people, events, and circumstances in your life.

Given that we all have unconscious limiting beliefs, how do you know which ones are driving you? Start by paying attention to your impact, and being ruthlessly honest with yourself about what you are achieving and experiencing in life. Where you see gaps between what's true in your life and what you want to be true in your life, you are likely to find limiting beliefs operating.

If you realize, through feedback or self-reflection, that you are demotivating people at work by micromanaging them, it's time to ask what story you're telling yourself that might be creating that behavior. Perhaps you believe others just aren't as capable as you, or if you want something done right, you have to do it yourself. It's a rich inquiry—paying attention to experiences and impact you're not happy with, and asking what beliefs might be at the root of them.

Or perhaps you reflect on why you're often late for meetings. Maybe it's because you believe it doesn't really matter if you're on time. Or you believe that others' time is less important than yours.

Choosing Empowering Narratives

As you get better at identifying limiting narratives, you're better positioned to choose ones that empower you. While it's not easy, it's definitely possible to change the stories that limit the quality of the impact and experience you're having.

Two things are essential to begin with. First, you have to believe you can. In other words, you must understand that your beliefs are not hard-wired into you. They are programs you can actually choose to change. Second is your commitment. All the insights in the world will not help you change stories you are not committed to changing.

Once you recognize that you can choose your beliefs, and you're committed to that, sometimes just bringing awareness to your stories is enough to change them. Exposing a belief can be enough to bring it out of the shadows of your unconscious and have you see its flimsiness. It's a bit like the sun burning away fog.

Or it may take more intense commitment and intentionality on your part. Some beliefs hold on more tightly than others, and sometimes the sun has to get pretty intense before the fog dissipates. In these cases, remind yourself what outcomes you're committed to creating in your life, and why. What's at stake? What makes the change worth it to you?

I spent many years believing that if I really wanted to make a difference in the world that I felt good about, and do work that was meaningful to me, I would always struggle to be financially successful. For most of that time, I had no clue that I was holding that story. When I finally became aware, it took some attention and discipline to notice the ways it was operating in me, and showing up in my life. It was particularly powerful to recognize that actually the opposite story was closer to the truth—and definitely more empowering—the story that being financially successful was part of, not antithetical to, making a meaningful difference in the world.

PARADIGM SHIFT ALERT
From: Choosing an empowering narrative is just putting a positive spin on reality.
To: Choosing an empowering narrative creates an empowered reality.

When you put your attention on changing your narratives about yourself, it can be helpful to notice that your stories are illustrated. In other words, how you think about yourself comes not only in words, but in images, which together make up your *self-image*. Your self-image is not a question of vanity, it's a question of success. Consider the possibility that the quality of your life and impact cannot exceed the potency of your self-image.

One of the most effective ways to upgrade your self-image is to identify with an actual image of a person you admire. Or perhaps it's a type of person. For example, you say to yourself, "I'm an athlete." "I'm a bold entrepreneur." "I'm an artist." "I'm a connector." "I'm a catalyst." You hold an image in mind of a person, or a role, that embodies the qualities that you want to bring more to the foreground in yourself.

When you connect your self-image to images you see around you, you are likely to find that you begin to take on the energy, mindsets, and behaviors of those types of people. For example, if you identify yourself as an *athlete*, and really see yourself that way, you will more naturally exercise and eat the way an athlete does. Or when you see yourself as a *sage*, you may be inspired to access and share more of the wisdom you have gained through your life experience.

I have a good friend who is a thought leader in his field. But it took him a while to acknowledge that fact to himself. It wasn't until he had written several books that he decided to hold the image of himself as an author and thought leader. As his change in self-image took hold in his mind, he began to make subtle but important shifts in his professional focus. He stopped traveling as much to teach and facilitate, and spent more time writing. He let others run more of the operations of his business, and put more energy into writing blogs and making short videos to get his ideas out to the world.

Changing your self-image takes awareness and commitment. It starts with listening more closely to the stories you tell yourself. You can do that by taking an honest look at what you are satisfied with, and what you are disappointed by in your life. Ask yourself what beliefs about yourself are creating what you are experiencing. Then ask yourself what stories would be more empowering than the ones you are currently believing, and notice what changes occur in your behavior and your experience based on your upgraded self-image.

You may find, despite how committed and intentional you are about choosing an empowering self-image, that there are times when you can't make it work. When you're in the grip of a story momentarily, ask yourself how your mood is feeding it. In those moments, your practice of Narrative may look like seeing what is needed to change your mood—a hug or a walk for example—and giving that to yourself.

There are limiting narratives that are pervasive in your experience. You may find yourself deep in a story that you know is limiting, and it just won't budge. For everyone—and I call these the big rocks in your stream—there are beliefs that are so constantly and firmly lodged in your psyche, that you need some help doing the heavy lifting. Your mind is worth liberating, and sometimes it's good to get help from a coach or therapist to do that.

With attention, commitment, and practice, you can see your stories and how they drive your behavior. To choose narratives about yourself and your world that empower you, is to take a stand for your own internal clarity, and the experience and impact you want to have in life.

ACTIVATION QUESTIONS
- What stories am I telling myself?
- How are my beliefs empowering or disempowering me in this moment?

Valuing Diverse Perspectives

While the practice of holding empowering narratives is primarily about you, your stories, and their impact on how you show up in the world, the practice of valuing diverse perspectives is primarily about how you engage in conversations with others. It is about co-creative conversation through honoring the validity and interplay of differing points of view. It is about being open minded while at the same time being able to assess and choose your own way of seeing something. It is being able to hold curiosity and conviction at the same time.

Letting Go of Having the One Right Answer

In the early 1990's, I had the privilege of attending a lecture by Oren Lyons, a prominent Native American elder who spoke internationally on behalf of Native tribes from the Northeastern U.S. Oren spoke compellingly about the decimation and oppression of Native Americans during the settling of North America by Europeans, and up to the present day at the hands of the U.S. government. What shocked me most though, was that at the end of his passionate lecture, he said "This is how I see it. I could be wrong...(pause), but I don't think so."

To me, Oren's words are the essence of Clarity as a discipline—"I could be wrong, but I don't think so." There is a combination of humility and conviction in that way of thinking—especially with high-stakes content. You choose and express a perspective—without invalidating others.

Have you ever been in a conversation in which you thought, "If only you understood me, you'd agree with me," and so keep trying to make your point? The idea that your view is the *right one* is a killer to co-creative conversation. But if you're like most people, your schooling and career have emphasized proving your intelligence and having the right answers. So the idea of letting go of thinking that your answer is the only right one can be a hard pill to swallow. It doesn't mean that you don't care about what's right, or have an opinion about right and wrong, or believe there's a right way to do something. It does mean that you recognize that your idea of what's right is *your idea*, and not *the only right one*. You likely have some part of the truth, but very unlikely have the whole truth.

In changing your mindset to becoming less attached to being right, you may want to start small. Simply acknowledge in a conversation that your point of view is *a perspective*, and not *the right answer*.

This applies to your inner dialogue as much as your conversation with others. Loosening your hold on your current perspective as the right one, and instead holding it as the one you are choosing at this time, enables you to consider other ways of thinking which may actually serve you better.

The more you practice valuing diverse perspectives, the more often you will realize there is rarely an objective right way to see something. There is instead the way you choose to see something. Rather than getting stuck on being right, you become discerning, which is choosing what to think and say, choosing what not to think and say, and being responsible for the consequences.

PARADIGM SHIFT ALERT
From: If you're right, it means other viewpoints are wrong.
To: Everyone has part of the truth and no one has the whole truth.

Drawing Out Diverse Perspectives

Letting go of being right makes your mind more open to diverse perspectives—both the ones you hear in your own head, and the ones you hear from others. The next step is to actively *value, invite,* and *truly listen* to points of view different from your own.

Valuing—Have you ever felt like someone has slammed the door on your idea, almost before it's out of your mouth? Have you ever been in a conversation where you felt stupid? And not because you didn't have expertise and ideas to share, but because the other person was dismissive. Perhaps they rolled their eyes or said "that's ridiculous," if only through body language.

Or perhaps you have been the person rolling your eyes. You

wouldn't be human if you hadn't thought to yourself, on more than one occasion, "That's a really stupid idea." And yet, it's what you do next that matters. Make the choice to truly value another's idea versus shutting it down.

This begins with acknowledging to yourself that everyone has a part of the truth, and no one has the whole truth. Recognize that there's some grain of brilliance in every idea, however small. So when you hear an idea that doesn't resonate with you, instead of immediately shooting it down, look for something you can value in it. You might explicitly acknowledge what you resonate with by saying something like, "What I like about that idea is..." Or, "the part that resonates with me, or makes sense to me, is..."

You don't have to agree with someone's point of view to value their perspective. When you can acknowledge something you appreciate about an idea, even if you don't fully agree with it, you can then talk about the parts you don't agree with and offer a different and/or complementary perspective, opening up the possibility for co-creative thinking and conversation to occur.

PARADIGM SHIFT ALERT
From: To value a perspective means to agree with it.
To: To value a perspective doesn't necessarily mean to agree with it. It means getting curious about the perspective and being willing and able to see its value in the eyes of those who hold it, as well as looking for its value for you.

Inviting—Over the years I have worked with a number of clients who resonate deeply with the idea of *being an invitation*. This is more than being approachable. It is creating an environment of openness that not only welcomes, but draws out a range of diverse perspectives onto the table.

To invite others begins with a mindset of valuing and practicing curiosity above certainty. Certainty makes you feel safe. But the problem with certainty is it makes your world smaller. You have to exclude, ignore, or refute anything that upsets what you know for sure. It takes a lot of energy to do that, and you miss out on important information and opportunity. It's like defending a small island. You can do it, but you're left stuck on a small island. In other words, you can keep defending what you know for sure, and in doing so you make yourself and your world smaller and more isolated.

Curiosity, on the other hand, enlarges you, enlarges your world, and is the quickest way to get unstuck. When you recognize that reality is largely a matter of perception—that things are as we *see* them, and not as fixed or black/white as most people think—you become more interested in your biases and how they are operating. You engage in more curiosity and less conflict.

To apply curiosity, ask powerful questions. Well-conceived questions open up the mental space for constructive conversation to occur—whether it's conversation between you and yourself, or conversation with another.

Asking great questions begins with unlearning what most of us have been taught from an early age—that being smart is having the answers. That's what tends to get rewarded most in school, and in business. We've been taught to think of questions in a context of lack—as in not having knowledge or understanding. But asking questions really should be held in a context of adding value. In other words, by asking a great question you could be contributing to an innovative idea or a greater wisdom emerging from a conversation—in a way that would not happen through sharing what you know, or as Mark Twain says, what you think you know.

Asking questions that truly invite diverse perspectives is an acquired skill. To help make your questions more powerful, ask yourself these questions:

- Are you genuinely curious?
- In asking the question, is your motivation to contribute, versus look smart or cross examine or disempower?
- Does your question help to clarify something?
- Are you willing to hear answers that you might not like?
- Is your question open ended?
- Is it a real question, or do you already have the answer?
- Does your question lead to greater understanding?
- When you ask a "why" question, is your aim to shed light on cause and effect, or to chastise and blame?
- What if you asked "what if?"
- Does your question create a learning opportunity?

Truly Listening—If you want to value and understand others' perspectives, truly listen. It's that simple. But everyone knows it's not that easy.

I have coached what seems like countless leaders who have been told they don't listen well. They have taken workshops and read books on active listening, and improve only marginally, sometimes getting proficient at fake listening, which most people recognize immediately. It's usually because they think listening is a skill. The idea that listening is a skill is only partially true. Actually, listening is less a skill, and more a mindset. You'll never be good at listening if you have the mindset that others aren't saying anything worth listening to, that your ideas are the ones that matter most, or that your spouse's day is less important than your business concerns.

Listening is a mindset of curiosity. It is a mindset of caring, appreciating, and valuing. If that's where you come from, you really don't have to work so hard at the skill of listening. Listening will come more naturally to you because you have the mindset that drives it.

Creating From Competing Points of View

While differing perspectives may clash, that doesn't have to signal a fight. Conflicting points of view don't have to create a zero-sum game. By avoiding a win/lose and right/wrong mindset, and instead honoring complexity and diversity in the world, competing points of view can lead to wonderfully creative ideas.

One of the origins of the word competition is the Latin verb *competere*, which denotes striving or seeking together, rather than against one another. It has a flavor of bringing out the best we each have to offer, instead of fighting for the upper hand. Conflict can have a similar flavor. We can look together at our differing perspectives, seeking their common ground.

Most of us though, have learned to pit our perspectives against each other, and one of the ways we try to win is to make the conversation cut and dry. One of my high school buddies used to get into heated philosophical arguments around the kitchen table with his mother. It would invariably come to the point where she would say in exasperation, "Son, you're just on the wrong side of the argument." While I chuckle looking back on it, my friend's mom's strategy has unfortunately become all too common in the world today—a strategy of making the other person wrong, claiming victory, and moving on. The problem with that approach is that it doesn't actually create clarity, but just ends the debate and deprives the conversation of its potential to be co-creative.

The opportunity present in competing or conflicting points of view is to engage in critical thinking together. But what often happens instead is that we engage in mutual criticism. Critical thinking together means evaluating perspectives (including your own), assessing data, learning from experience, being aware of the impact of beliefs and perceptions, and drawing conclusions—all for the sake of creating value through the conversation. Criticism, on the other hand, is about de-valuing through the conversation—de-valuing another's ideas or arguments, and if that doesn't get you the win, de-valuing the other person. While critical thinking can open up opportunities for creative ideas to emerge in a conversation, criticism tends to shut the door on them.

Critical thinking has an energy of alertness. Instead of getting mentally sleepy, it is staying awake to what's really going on in a thought process or conversation. Being intensely awake can at times add *edge* to the conversation—edge in the form of shooting holes in an argument, or edge in the form of playing devil's advocate. The key is to make this edginess a respectful part of the process of arriving at the most effective, innovative, or useful ideas possible—and to *flag it* as such. To flag it literally means saying something like, "I appreciate your perspective, and allow me to play devil's advocate for a moment." Or, "For the sake of getting to the best strategy, let's debate this."

There can be an empowering place for edgy intellectual dueling in valuing diverse perspectives. Debate can be highly energizing and co-creative when you invite others into it, rather than attack them with it. Inviting into debate is like calling someone to come out and play. It can expand and elevate the creative quality of the conversation. On the other hand, using debate as a form of attack can have a bullying effect, which takes potential creative thinking out of the conversation.

Expanding Your Vision

Being a visionary person and leader is much more than having big goals. It is a practice of expanding your ability to look at the past, present, and future in ways that empower.

Influential German philosopher Arthur Schopenhauer is reported to have said, "Every man takes the limits of his own field of vision for the limits of the world." Consider the notion that you limit or expand your potential—what you can do, and who you can be in the world—through your willingness and ability to expand and clarify your field of vision.

You are always creating your experience of life, and your results in life, from the way you see the world—whether you are doing this consciously or not. To become conscious about how you view the full spectrum of experience—the past, present, and future—is possibly the most productive use of your mind. I call this *full-spectrum vision.*

Full-spectrum vision involves three things: learning from the past, viewing the present in a way that creates opportunity, and imagining a desired future. To learn from the past and see present opportunity are essential platforms for imagining a future that is both possible and compelling.

This *full-spectrum* practice of vision applies to your self-development as much as to your world. It's seeing with clear eyes who you have been, who you are, and who you are becoming.

Learning From the Past

Looking in the rear-view mirror is important—with the right mindset. While it's not creative or productive to ruminate, it is helpful to see the past as clearly as possible, and learn from it in a way that enables you to refine the way you see yourself and your world.

Failures and disappointments in the past are powerful opportunities to learn in a way that empowers you to create something different, rather than in a way that is reactive and only creates more reactivity. For example, a reactive approach to learning from an upsetting interaction in a relationship might sound like, "I'm never to talking to that jerk again." Creative learning might sound like, "Hmm, I wonder what happened in that interaction—I wonder how I contributed to the upset, and what I can do differently next time."

In a conversation with an acquaintance about her recent divorce, she described all the ways her husband was abusive and took advantage of her. The learning she took away was to never get married again. While never getting married again is certainly a valid option, I suspect her learning could have been something entirely different. If she were to look deeply into what she contributed to creating the dysfunctional relationship, while not ignoring or denying the impact her husband had on her, perhaps she would come away with important insights to apply to future relationships— and thus truly learn.

One of the most powerful ways to learn in a way that changes you is to ask, "Why?" Not in order to self-criticize or find blame, but to understand what is creating your experience. And not, "Why is this happening to me?"—which would be an unproductive and disempowering victim stance—but, "Why am I creating (or re-creating) this experience?" When you take yourself through that reflective process, you can't help but discover mindsets and behaviors that are worn out, and need replacing.

As a leader on a team or in an organization, when things go wrong, ask, "Why?" in order to learn, not so that you can find the right person to blame. That bears repeating. Way too often, leaders are oriented toward blame. When we fall off the horse, so to speak—when we make mistakes—blame tends to keep us lying bruised on the ground. Learning puts us back in the saddle. In other words, blame tends to diminish our desire and capability to do better, while learning tends to build it.

PARADIGM SHIFT ALERT
From: Asking why a breakdown occurred always leads to improvement.
To: Asking why a breakdown occurred can help generate something better when it comes from true curiosity and a desire to learn, rather than seeking to blame and shame.

Focusing on Present Opportunity

Your view of what's going on in the here and now is most creative when you're focused on opportunity—which has several elements to it. The first is *seeing the big picture*—insight into a whole "ecosystem" (forest for the trees), whether it's a business market, the healthcare system, or your marriage, and bringing that understanding to bear on how you operate and what you see as possible. That includes bringing your thought process to bear on the kind of person you have the opportunity to be in order to be equal to the challenges of your environment.

Second is seeing *what's working*. This helps you capitalize on the fact that what you focus on, you get more of. When you focus your attention on what's working and what you're doing well, the positive energy you generate gives you greater confidence and capability to deal with problems when they arise. This doesn't mean that you ignore failure *and* disappointment as they are occurring, but it does mean you see the difficulty in those problem moments through a mindset of curiosity about the opportunity in them.

One specific way of combining your ability to see what's working with your ability to see the big picture is to *see the big in people*, which means seeing their best, and intuiting their potential, especially when they cannot see it themselves. Insight into the big in someone has a similar impact as focusing on what's working. You tend to get more of what you see. And when you see the big picture for someone, it helps them to not get bogged down in the small stuff, and to see what's possible. Seeing the big is a gift that most people respond well to by living up to the potential you see in them.

A third element of opportunity-focus is *seeing context*. You see the "why" or "what for" of important conversations and initiatives. Like, "Are we having this conversation in the context of committed partnership, or dating?" Or, "Is our strategy geared more toward short-term or long-term?" When you see the context clearly, what is both desirable and possible to create shows up in sharper relief as well.

A final element is *seeing the seeds of the future*—anticipating where current trends may lead, including the trends of your own behaviors—the ones that occur over and over. Where are the trends leading, do you like what you see, and what kinds of possibilities are they pointing to?

In my twenties, I was an environmental educator with a particular expertise in birds of prey. I had trained myself to recognize at a glance a wide range of hawks, owls and other raptors. To this day, I see hawks flying or perched along the roadways where most people miss them. My subconscious mind is always on the lookout, and my gaze instinctually picks up what my mind knows to look for. It's the same with opportunity. When you've trained your mind to look for it, you more easily and naturally see it.

PARADIGM SHIFT ALERT
From: The word "opportunity" is a politically correct reference to a deficiency or problem.
To: Seeing the world as full of "opportunity" leads to substantially different results than seeing the world as full of problems.

Imagining What Can Be

In 1961, President John F. Kennedy addressed the US Congress with these words: "I believe that this nation should commit itself to achieving the goal, before this decade is out, of landing a man on the moon and returning him safely to the earth. No single space project in this period will be more impressive to mankind, or more important for the long-range exploration of space."

Leadership theorists often hold up Kennedy's words as an example of a powerful future vision, and the impact it can have.

An effective future vision lays down tracks. It paints an image, through words and images, of a state of being, physical thing, relationship, or anything you want to create, change, or expand in your life. Once you have a clear picture, you *hold it in your mind's eye* as if it were real and true right now. As you hold the image, you imagine what it would *feel* like to experience that vision as reality right now.

As a competitive swimmer in secondary school, I was lucky enough to have a coach who taught me to use visioning to improve my performance. In the evening before each swim meet, I would find a comfortable place to lie on my back (my event was backstroke)—usually on my bed or even in the bathtub—and spend several minutes going over the entire race in my mind's eye. I would imagine the feeling in my body of the stroke technique and the relaxed intensity needed to be at my best in the pool.

Forty years later, there are now volumes of information drawing on fields as wide-ranging as quantum physics and neurobiology to explain the principles behind the practice of visioning. One of the most fundamental concepts is that how we see things in our minds has a huge impact on how we actually experience them. First, because your perception—or seeing—is your experience. And second, because your mental activity is a kind of gravitational force, attracting to you people, opportunities, and experiences; and even influencing the way your cells function. Because you always have mental activity, and it is always attracting something, there is wisdom and power in using your mind to intentionally envision what you *want* to create, rather than allowing random thoughts to create a random life.

This mental activity of using vision as an intentionally creative force is not only powerful in your own life, but also in leading others. You may be the *visionary* who inspires a whole community, team, organization, or family to achieve something together. Or you may facilitate a collective process. While Kennedy articulated a vision to the world, he didn't dream it up alone and impose it on an entire community of scientists, engineers, and workers. His closest advisors spent weeks polling leaders in the military, industry, and space exploration. He engaged all kinds of people in conversations about what they thought was possible, and what they thought was worthy of intense focus and effort. Sometimes it is the quality of the collective visioning conversation that determines the success of the initiative. When people are involved in the visioning process in an effective way, they have a greater stake in the outcome.

PARADIGM SHIFT ALERT
From: Future-vision is a nice-sounding sentence to put on a website or hang on a wall in your corporate headquarters.
To: Future-vision is not an outcome, but an ongoing practice of imagining the future you want to create.

ACTIVATION QUESTIONS
- Am I blaming or learning something?
- How is the quality of my vision creating my experience?

Judgment and Confusion

(The Reactive Patterns of Clarity)

For Clarity, being judgmental is a distortion of the real thing. Judgment can look like Clarity, but is actually a façade of it.

Clarity repressed is *confusion*. As an attempt to keep from being judgmental, or simply out of fear of choosing a point of view and taking a stand, we can default to confusion. When we're confused, we may tell ourselves it means we're being open minded and curious, when we're actually being mentally lazy.

Remember, as you read about judgment and confusion, that we all are subject to reactivity from time to time through lack of awareness and intention. The inner adventure is to catch ourselves in reaction, and in the spirit of radical responsibility, choose the Discipline over the distortion or repression.

Judgment (Clarity Distorted)

Judgment can mean choosing a point of view or making a clear decision. However, in the context of distortions, we're talking about being judgmental—a kind of closed-minded certainty that resembles Clarity, but isn't. Being judgmental has a black and white flavor, a quality of being cut and dry, that can be mistaken for being clear, but is actually a resistance to the radical responsibility of Clarity—resisting the thoughtfulness, reflection, and discernment it takes to keep an open mind while also choosing a point of view.

The being right syndrome—*Would you rather be right, or be in relationship?* Or more specifically, in *co-creative* relationship. It's amazing how often we seem more interested in our point of view being right than in having relationships that work and conversations that are generative. In order for you to be right, the other person has to be wrong, which means rather than mutual exploration, you're fighting for the upper hand. You become adversarial rather than co-creative. Insisting on being right impedes productive thinking, and instead perpetuates tired and familiar conflicts.

I notice that when I insist on being right about something—whether it's which route to take to the grocery store, or what strategy to use in working with a leadership team—I am actually being small-minded, rather than the confident and decisive person I think I'm being. Insisting that I'm right makes me less open to a different perspective, and therefore less actively engaged in the relationship.

Even if you don't voice how right you think you are, and how wrong you think another point of view is, it's hard to mask it. Your right/wrong stance tends to leak out in body language—eye-rolling, for example—or a condescending tone that diminishes another person or group or something they've done or believe in.

Attachment to being right is one way that our reactive minds try to validate our own thinking, and protect us from the ambiguities and complexities of our world. It isn't easy to let go of. It takes being willing to challenge your most firmly held beliefs about what and/or who is right and wrong. Which doesn't mean that you stop being committed to *doing the right thing*. But it does mean recognizing that doing the *right thing* is a choice you make for you, not the *right* choice for everyone. As you see that, you begin to stop framing your conversations in terms of *right and wrong*—but rather focus on what you choose to think, what others choose to think, the stands you choose to take, the impact of your thoughts and stands, and what you can learn in the process.

Breaking the being-right syndrome doesn't mean that you never take an absolute stand on what you believe is right and wrong. But it does mean you loosen your grip on making absolute judgments. You challenge yourself when you hear yourself thinking or communicating in ways that disrespect the many ambiguities of life and the rich conversations to be found in all its complexity.

Criticism versus critical thinking—One of the more toxic ways judgment shows up is criticism, which is different from thinking critically or making an argument for or against a perspective. Criticism has a tone of disrespect, and often personal attack—putting someone down for who they are, what they do, or what they believe. While that tone is obviously toxic to others, in a more subtle way it is toxic to ourselves as well. It is like swallowing the poison that we think is only going outward.

While criticism is toxic, let's recognize that it's also very normal. It happens everywhere, and all the time. But what would happen if we released the world from our criticism? Consider the possibility that in dropping the habit of criticism, we not only free other people, situations and things, we free ourselves as well from swallowing the toxicity it carries.

Blame versus learning—Blame is certainly warranted in the world of legality and crime. In that context, it may rightly come with punishment and/or restitution. There are other circumstances as well, in which placing blame is important for identifying where accountability lies, and for setting something right.

The trouble occurs when we start living from a blame mindset—when placing blame, and finding ways to punish, becomes our default position in life. This is when blame becomes a flavor of judgment. It's easy to allow blame to become a reaction that is the rule, instead of a carefully chosen response to certain circumstances. As a reaction, blame perpetuates adversarial conversations instead of co-creative ones. It tends to close down the creative dialogue that could lead to learning and productive change.

When you choose a learning mindset, when things go wrong,

you ask what you can learn, and how you can create a better outcome the next time, rather than ask who you can punish.

PARADIGM SHIFT ALERT
From: Criticism and blame clarify things.
To: Criticism and blame limit critical thinking, clear communication, and co-creative learning.

Writing people off—Both criticism and blame can lead to writing people off. We see this everywhere, from marital spats to global conflicts. When you write someone off, you make them wrong in general, or worse yet, bad in general. That means you can stop being open to the merit of their ideas and actions in the moment, which is convenient because then you don't have to try to understand them or perhaps do the hard work of forgiveness. In order to write someone off, you have to make up an airtight narrative about them, and then see them through the lens of your beliefs about them. It creates a closed loop of self-fulfilling prophecy.

It's possible, and more common than you might think, to write yourself off as well—through your self-judgments. Judgment turned inward as a harsh self-critic, or blaming yourself habitually, can be as detrimental to your relationships as judging others.

On the other end of the spectrum from writing someone off, is putting them on a pedestal. Instead of judging people as wrong and bad, we put them on pedestals and see them through a do-no-wrong lens. When someone, or some organization or belief system, can do no wrong in your eyes, you are just as blind as when you criticize and judge harshly.

Confusion (Clarity Repressed)

Confusion is Clarity repressed. Instead of knowing for sure, like judgment, it's refusing to know. Or it can be denying what you do know. It may look like being open minded, but is actually a version of closed-mindedness because it is fundamentally a stance of resistance. Confusion can be a smokescreen for not being willing to discern, think critically, assign accountability, or communicate clearly—for not being willing to take on the responsibility that comes with choosing a point of view.

For example, at a particular point in her life, a friend of mine kept saying that she was very confused about what direction to go in her career. It seemed at the time like a perfectly legitimate state of mind, given the complexity of options and factors to weigh. And yet, something didn't quite ring true. The breakthrough for her was realizing that she had been reluctant to acknowledge and follow through on what she already knew about her strengths, her career path, and the steps she needed to take.

Confusion as a repression of Clarity is different from not understanding something—which can occur when there is a lack of clear communication, more complexity than you can process, or simply recognizing that the answer isn't clear yet. As a repression, confusion is avoiding clear thought. It is a mind resistant to, or backing away from, drawing conclusions, being discerning, and making decisions.

Confusion can subtly be another way of writing someone off. By avoiding thoughtful assessment of someone's talents, motivations, or ideas, you are choosing not to see them. This is a kind of confusion, or repression of clarity; and ironically, it can be caused by a fear of being closed-minded and judgmental and hurting someone. Or, it may be caused by an unwillingness to deal with the complexity, or potential conflict, of differing points of view.

PARADIGM SHIFT ALERT
From: Confusion stems from being too open-minded.
To: Confusion is a version of closed-mindedness because it is fundamentally a resistance to clear thinking
and discernment.

✦

ACTIVATION QUESTIONS
- In what way(s) am I being critical or judgmental?
- What am I pretending not to know?

Chapter 6 Summary Points

Clarity is seeing the world and yourself with an open and discerning mind. It is a discipline of living in the synergy of curiosity and conviction. It is also using your mind not only to understand your world, but also to create it.

Holding Empowering Narratives
Holding empowering narratives is listening to your internal dialogue, and choosing the stories you want to give space and credence to in your own mind. It is identifying your limiting beliefs, and choosing empowering ones.

Valuing Diverse Perspectives
The practice of valuing diverse perspectives is letting go of insisting that you are right and others are wrong, while also giving yourself permission to have a strong point of view. You honor perspectives other than your own, ask powerful questions to elevate conversations, and embrace conflict for its creative value.

Expanding Your Vision
Full-spectrum visioning is seeing clearly what has been, what is, and what can be. You see the past in a way that enables transformation, assess the present for what it offers, and see the future for what is possible in it. When you see possibility—and when you imagine yourself, your relationships, and your world as you want them to be—your vision lays down tracks for your creative energy to follow.

Judgment and Confusion
Being judgmental is a distorted attempt at Clarity. It is blame, criticism, and attachment to having the one right view. Confusion is Clarity repressed—it's abdicating mental acuity and discernment.

Chapter 6 Journaling

Beliefs or narratives I hold that empower me are...

Beliefs or narratives I hold that disempower me are...

A narrative I am ready to change or simply stop telling myself is...

What's hard about letting go of being right is...

I could engage with conflict more effectively by...

Something I want to manifest more of in my life right now (e.g., satisfying relationship, great home environment, work I love, etc) is...

My vision of it—in other words, how it would ideally look—is...

I am judgmental when...

The cost to me and others of being judgmental is...

To be less judgmental, I need to...

CLARITY
Holding Empowering Narratives
Valuing Diverse Perspectives
Expanding Your Vision

INTEGRITY
Being Honest
Bringing Excellence
Caring for Your
Physical World

Radical
Responsibility

INSPIRATION
Claiming Your Core Identity
Sourcing from Beauty
Activating Enthusiam

COURAGE
Leaning In
Braving Connection
Living in Appreciation

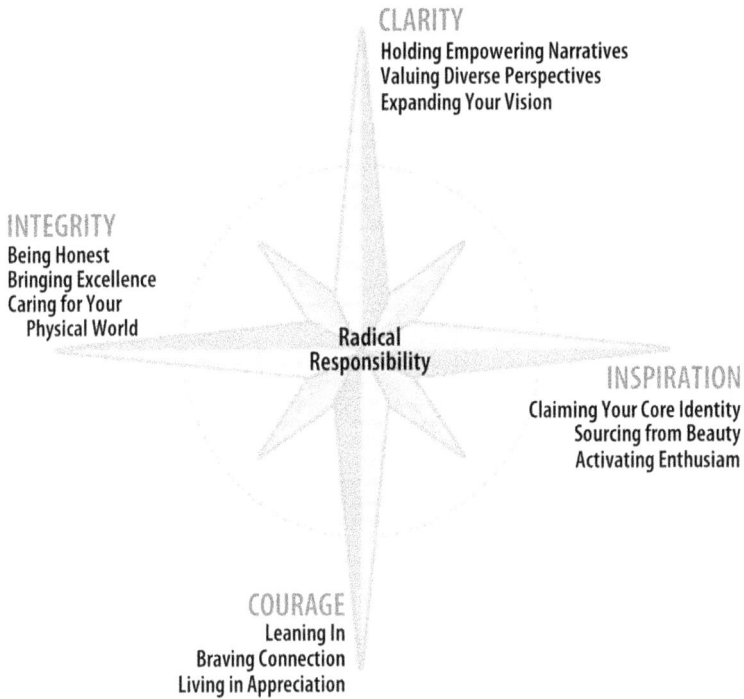

Disciplines and Core Practices Review

Before moving on to the final chapter, in which we look at the Four Disciplines as a whole, take a moment to review the Core Practices.

• What connections do you see among them?

• What ways do they complement each other to help you become a more balanced, integrated, and whole human being?

~ Chapter Seven ~

Balance and Wholeness

EACH OF THE FOUR DISCIPLINES stands alone as an invitation to a powerful relationship with a core aspect of yourself. Together, the Disciplines invite inner balance—a balance of the spiritual, physical, emotional and mental elements of what it means to be human, and what it means to embrace leadership and life as a sacred trust.

Life is always inviting us to grow and evolve, and as you embrace Life's calling, consider an important paradox. On one hand, you are already whole—there is nothing about you that needs to be fixed. At the same time, there is always more of that **wholeness to reveal**, the way a sculptor chips away stone to reveal the beauty of the image underneath his chisel.

In addition to revealing, there are opportunities to *restore* wholeness and balance, which are ways of saying *to heal*. To acknowledge the ways we have been wounded in life, recognize there is an innate wholeness underneath the wounding, and then find ways to strengthen and restore that innate balance and wholeness of being.

The Disciplines are one way, one path, to strengthen and restore our innate wholeness. They are powerful individually. And

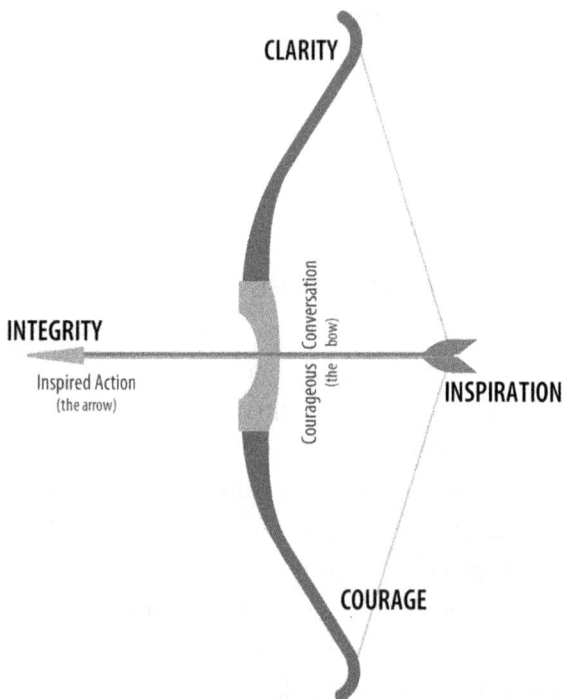

CLARITY

Courageous Conversation
(the bow)

INTEGRITY

Inspired Action
(the arrow)

INSPIRATION

COURAGE

A metaphor for the way we are designed to be creative forces in the world is the dynamic interaction of a bow and arrow.

even more potent together—constellating an integrated whole that transcends the sum of the parts. They remind you of the whole human being that you are, and offer a pathway to optimum enjoyment of your life and optimal impact in it.

An Integrating Metaphor

Let's look at the Disciplines together through the lens of an integrating metaphor—an image of wholeness you can hold in your mind.

The metaphor points to the beauty and power of how we are designed as human beings. We are built to create, but not just anything. We're built to manifest in ways that reflect our best selves. We're meant to bring things into form in the physical world that reflect more than random acts of busyness, or accumulation, but are inspired by our sense of what is good, noble, and beautiful. We are designed to create things and experiences that have value and meaning to us and make our presence on the planet more life-affirming.

Inspired Action

The arrow is Inspired Action, the balanced dynamic between Inspiration and Integrity. Whether it's providing for the family and caring for the children, or making a product or providing a service, Integrity is most fundamentally about *following through* on what *inspires* you—your values, purpose, and connection to imagination and beauty. Integrity is about taking the *action* necessary to bring your life into alignment with your highest intentions.

The arrow of Inspired Action is our natural inclination to manifest things and experiences that have meaning—things and experiences of beauty and excellence. Without the feathers (Inspiration) on the arrow, the flight is erratic and lacks direction. Without the point (Integrity), the arrow falls flat.

Inspiration is most essentially our devotion to life. Without the force of that devotion our will, our work, and our actions all have a kind of emptiness. Devotion infuses what we do in life with the potency of meaning.

Courageous Conversation

In the metaphor of the bow and arrow, the bow is *Courageous Conversation*—heart and mind in balanced and integrated connection.

There is a tendency, especially in Western culture, to think of the heart and mind as enemies. Courageous conversation is the opposite of that. It is the heart and mind in synch, each enhancing the other.

Courageous conversation is thinking and communicating with your heart open—being willing to stand in the fire of whatever emotions come up in relation to the thoughts in your head or the words being said. To deny the impact of emotion on your thinking is quite frankly naïve. To let emotion completely override your thinking or dictate the words that come out of your mouth, is irresponsible.

There are times when I think, "I don't have the heart for this conversation." Sometimes that means that I don't want to spend the emotional energy I anticipate the conversation will take. Other times, it means that I'm afraid to have the conversation because I anticipate it will evoke emotions—for me, for the other person, or both—that are uncomfortable.

And this isn't only when the conversation is with someone else, or in a team or community context. It can also be when the conversation is just between you and yourself. There are conversations with ourselves that feel so difficult that we want to avoid them.

Courage—or having the heart to do something difficult that is meaningful to you—is what enables you to have the tough, or downright painful, conversations—whether with yourself or others. Your heart-strength—your courage—enables you to be in the conversation. It also enables you to do it skillfully. You only have to look at the distortion of Courage, which is Defensiveness, to see what difference Courage makes to the skill you bring to a conversation. Defensiveness is one of the most obvious and damaging ways to be unskillful.

You might astutely ask what the difference is between standing up for yourself and being defensive. The difference is entirely about your intent, which can often be subconscious. Is your intent to harm or punish? Or is it to keep your heart and mind open? Defensiveness and withdrawing are both about harming or punishing. You may use the sharpness of your mind to cut someone to pieces, or you can cut off from them. Neither are courageous conversation. Bringing Courage to your conversations is about keeping your heart open in those interactions, even when it feels vulnerable to do so.

On the other side of the coin from the head overruling the heart, is when the reverse is occurring—when your emotions are leading, but your mind is not tracking. Perhaps you've allowed a flood of emotion to drown out your thought processes. This is also antithetical to courageous conversation. An open heart does not mean runaway emotion. It's not a license for your thoughts and words to go places you later wish they hadn't.

PARADIGM SHIFT ALERT
From: The head and heart are at odds with each other.
To: The head and heart are a dynamic duo to help you navigate life effectively.

Being wholehearted is Courage. Being open and discerning is Clarity. This synergy of heart and mind enables the courageous conversations critical to your ability to achieve great things in life.

Bow and Arrow:
Courageous Conversation Enabling Inspired Action

The bow and arrow metaphor is a natural flow—from Inspiration to Integrity, strengthened and balanced by the dynamic synergy of Courage and Clarity.

When your mind is clear, and your heart is open and whole, you enhance the combined power of an alive spirit and your ability to be true. Inspired action needs courageous conversation. The strength or weakness of the bow liberates or limits the flight of the arrow.

The metaphor of bow and arrow can be a powerful force in your daily life. Your day doesn't happen to you. You create it with your choices, including the energy, thoughts, and emotions you bring to whatever you do. Consider guiding your choices with two mantras: inspired action and courageous conversation.

ACTIVATION QUESTIONS
- Are my actions today connected to my most inspired self?
- What is the most courageous thing I can communicate today?

One Word

Back to the summer of 1968. I was 9, at an overnight summer camp in Maine. As darkness settled over the council ring under towering white pines, I sat transfixed by the "Four Winds" as they spoke fiercely of the qualities they expected us to live at camp. I had no idea at that age how privileged I was to be there. I do now. Fifty years later, the rocky trails through the forest, the soft water of the lake, the smell of pine and spruce, are all etched deeply into my body and soul. Throughout my childhood, teens, and into my twenties, I spent most of my summers in Maine as a camper and counselor. And I returned numerous times for the end-of-season family/adult camp week. It was during one of those adult weeks that I started writing this book while sitting on a deck overlooking the lake, watching loons and bald eagles hunt for fish.

I continued going back to Maine for week-long writing retreats. On one of those retreats, on a sunny afternoon having lunch with a small group of college-age counselors, the conversation came around to my writing. One of the counselors asked me what I thought was the most important quality for great leadership. It was a simple question, and you'd think I'd have an immediate answer. But in twenty years as an executive coach and leadership educator, I had never boiled it down to one quality. What came out of my mouth in that moment, and out of my gut really, was *"humility."*

Humility, not in the sense of diminishing or downplaying yourself. But humility in the sense of acknowledging that your gifts are gifts—an expression of the generosity of life. Humility in the sense that you are the steward of your own gifts and greatness, privileged to be able to offer yourself generously to the world.

This kind of humility is true power. Not the power that insists that the world serve you, but your power to be of service in the world.

PARADIGM SHIFT ALERT

From: Humility means diminishing yourself and being subservient.

To: Humility means honoring what is noble in yourself and how you want to be of service in the world.

Humility is the one factor that most distinguishes a Discipline (Inspiration, Integrity, etc.) from a reactive pattern (arrogance, passiveness, defensiveness, etc).

For example, humility-infused Inspiration is you attuning to your spirit for the sake of greater aliveness and sense of purpose. But without humility, what could be Inspiration becomes arrogance, a distortion that elevates human status over human spirit.

Integrity is living out your commitment to truth and excellence in the world around you, but when humility drops out of the equation, you're living more in the reactive patterns of control or passiveness—trying to make the world around you bend to your will (control), or neglecting to activate your will (passiveness).

As an essential aspect of Courage, humility is a willingness to expose your heart to the world, rather than protecting it from the world, as we do in the reactive patterns of defensiveness and withdrawal.

The Discipline of Clarity infused with humility makes you aware and discerning in your points of view without making others wrong or bad in theirs.

We are contextual beings. In other words, everything we do is influenced by the contexts we hold. What's your context for leadership? Perhaps it's the idea that leaders are in privileged positions of authority, with the right to tell others what to do. Or instead, that leadership is a sacred trust, characterized by humility and exercising true power. What's your context for marriage? Perhaps it's the idea that marriage is a series of compromises you are resigned to. Or that marriage is a commitment between two people who love each other to support one another in their growth as human beings. What's your context for human presence on the planet? Perhaps it's to be stewards of the natural world. Or to use up what Nature provides because you think humans won't be around much longer anyway.

There are many examples of context, within which our thoughts, feelings, and actions make sense. Humility is a powerful context. It is the key to activating the conscious leader in yourself. This potent context will do more than anything else to enhance the power of your impact, and the way you experience life.

Each of the summer-camp seasons spent in Maine ended with a final council fire. At that gathering, as night fell across the lake and the fire began to die down, the master of ceremonies concluded the camp season by saying, "I leave with you a word. That word is .... Use it well". We were instructed to do our utmost to be faithful to that one word in our lives over the fall, winter, and spring months until we returned the next summer to the deep woods and rocky shores of Long Lake.

In conclusion to this book, I leave with you a word. That word is *humility*.

Blessings on your journey!

Gratitude

THIS BOOK HAS EMERGED from my own personal and professional journey through life. So, while I will not attempt to mention all the people who have been important to me and, thus, contributors to this book, I do want to mention a few. My grandmother, Guin Rich, who unconditionally loved me, believed in me, and supported me, no matter what crazy path I chose do go down. My mother, Shelley Burke, who has championed the philosopher and writer in me, and who has shown up time and time again to both celebrate my wins and provide comfort and support in my struggles. My father, Wally Miller, who has loved me unconditionally and shown me what it looks like to chart one's own path. My son Ryan—the soulful, creative, and passionate being that he is—for all the joy and learning that our father/son relationship has offered.

Deep gratitude to my men's group—Andrew, Andy, Andy, Chris, and Eric—who have for 18 years challenged and inspired me to keep growing into the fullest expression of the man, husband, father, and professional I want to be.

I am grateful to my clients. Thank you for the devotion and curiosity it takes to open yourself to transformations big and small. Thank you for your stories and your trust. Thank you for teaching me about inspiration, integrity, courage, and clarity.

Some of the most profound teachers in my life are people I have never met personally, though I have had rich internal conversations with their written work. Among the most influential are Brené Brown, Peter Senge, Parker Palmer, Theodore Roszak, Margaret Wheatley, David Whyte, and Ken Wilber.

I have also been extremely blessed to know and work personally with some of the wisest and most skilled teachers in the fields of leadership and evolving human consciousness. I am deeply grateful to Karen and Henry Kimsey-House, founders of the co-active way of leadership and coaching. To Steven Foster and Meredith Little, founders of the School of Lost Borders. To WhiteEagle Woman, Keeper of the Delicate Lodge. To Faith Fuller and Marita Fridjohn, founders of CRR Global. To Craig Ross and Steven Vannoy, founders of Verus Global. To Debra Silverman, astrologer and psychotherapist. And to Barbara Cecil, creator of The Symbols Way. You have all given me immense gifts personally, and contributed profoundly to the creative emergence of the Four Disciplines.

To Robert Krenza, CEO of BlackWolf Consultants, my wholehearted gratitude for your wise counsel, generous partnering, and the flow of opportunity you have opened up for the Four Disciplines to make an impact on the lives of leaders around the world.

A huge thank you to my editor, John Kadlecek—for your thoughtful guidance, for seeing and refining the writer in me, and for keeping me on track.

Finally, I am profoundly grateful to my wife Sandra Visser. Thank you for recognizing the depth of my calling to write, believing in my message, and so generously giving of yourself to help bring this book to fruition. I will be forever grateful to you for your unwavering encouragement, thought partnership, love, and support—in life, and in the creative process of *A Sacred Trust*.

Recommended Reading

THE FOLLOWING BOOKS are my "top-20-list." It was hard to whittle the list down, but these are the books that, over the past 45 years, have had the most profound influence on my life. My gratitude to their authors is amplified by the much fuller appreciation I now have for the labor of love that is required to put one's ideas out into the world.

A Return to Love: Reflections on the Principles of A Course in Miracles, Marianne Williamson

A Simpler Way, Margaret J. Wheatley and Myron Kellner-Rogers

Awakened Leadership: Beyond Self-Mastery, Alan E. Shelton

Callings: Finding and Following an Authentic Life, Gregg Levoy

Daring Greatly: How the Courage to be Vulnerable Transforms the Way We Live, Love, Parent, and Lead, Brené Brown, Ph.D., LMSW

King, Warrior, Magician, Lover: Rediscovering the Archetypes of the Mature Masculine, Robert Moore and Douglas Gillette

Person/Planet*: The Creative Disintegration of Industrial Society*, Theodore Roszak

Presence*: Human Purpose and the Field of the Future*, Peter Senge, et. al.

Quantum Leaps*: Seven Skills for Workplace ReCreation*, Charlotte Shelton

Success with Soul*: New Insights to Achieving Success with Real Meaning*, Doris Pozzi and Stephen Williams

The Answer to How is Yes*: Acting on What Matters*, Peter Block

The Artist's Way*: A Spiritual Path to Higher Creativity*, Julia Cameron

The Corporate Mystic*: A Guidebook for Visionaries with their Feet on the Ground*, Gay Hendricks, Ph.D. and Kate Ludeman, Ph.D.

The Courage to Teach*: Exploring the Inner Landscape of a Teacher's Life*, Parker Palmer

The Four Agreements*: A Practical Guide to Personal Freedom*, Don Miguel Ruiz

The Heart Aroused*: Poetry and the Preservation of the Soul in Corporate America*, David Whyte

The Invitation, Oriah Mountain Dreamer

The Magic of Conflict*: Turning a Life of Work into a Work of Art*, Thomas F. Crum

The Web of Life*: A New Scientific Understanding of Living Systems*, Fritjof Capra

Wisdom at Work*: The Awakening of Consciousness in the Workplace*, Lee Davidson, Ph.D.

About the Author

BURKE MILLER is an executive coach and leadership educator. He has been an ardent explorer of philosophy, psychology, leadership, and human development for more than 45 years.

Burke began his career as an environmental and experiential educator. In his mid-thirties, he discovered environmental philosophy and ecopsychology. It was through his master's thesis work, on environmental consciousness, that Burke entered the field of leadership development—making a direct link between how we show up as human beings with one another and our planet, and how we lead in organizations. From the late 1990's onward, Burke has been a deeply committed student of leadership, serving leaders in traditional ways like executive coaching and teaching week-long leadership seminars, to non-traditional ways, including executive "wisdom quests"—taking clients into the mountains of Colorado for deep explorations of their leadership fulfillment and impact.

Burke's clients span the professional spectrum, from pioneers in education reform, to non-profit directors, to C-suite executives in multi-billion dollar global companies. He has had the privilege to coach, teach, and facilitate extensively internationally, working with leaders throughout the Americas, Europe, Australia, New Zealand, China, Russia, India and Japan for multinational clients including Mars, Owens-Illinois, Kellogg, Proctor and Gamble, Accenture, BBDO, Publicis, Nestle, and Mazda.

Among his clients, Burke is known for his warm presence, depth of wisdom, and way of listening and communicating that is inspiring, provocative, compassionate, and direct. He creates the combination of safety and challenge that leaders need to move out of their comfort zones into new ways of thinking and being.

Burke's formal education includes an MA from Antioch University and a BA from Williams College. He has extensive formal training, experience, and mastery in educational design; and advanced coaching and leadership development training from a variety of organizations, including the Coaches Training Institute and The Leadership Circle.

A Sacred Trust draws not only on twenty years of Burke's experience in the leadership field, but also on his life-long and passionate study of spiritual and psychological wisdom—a personal journey that has kept bringing him back to a fourfold nature-based way of understanding what it means to be a human being. *The Four Disciplines of Conscious Leadership* framework is an integrated, holistic, and comprehensive synthesis of that journey.

Burke is based in Boulder, Colorado, where he has lived for more than thirty years, surrounded by the beauty of the mountains, and enjoying skiing, hiking, and swimming year round.

Contact the author via: www.linkedin.com/in/burke999/